THE LITTLE BOOK OF

Restorative Justice
for
Colleges and Universities

SECOND EDITION

Repairing Harm and Rebuilding Trust in Response to Student Misconduct

DAVID R. KARP

FOREWORD BY MARILYN ARMOUR

Good Books

New York, New York

The Little Books of Justice & Peacebuilding present, in highly accessible form, key concepts and practices from the fields of restorative justice, conflict transformation, and peacebuilding. Written by leaders in these fields, they are designed for practitioners, students, and anyone interested in justice, peace, and conflict resolution.
The Little Books of Justice & Peacebuilding series is a cooperative effort between the Center for Justice and Peacebuilding of Eastern Mennonite University (Howard Zehr, Series General Editor) and publisher Good Books.

Cover photograph by Howard Zehr

Cover Design by Cliff Snyder

Page Design by Mike Bond

THE LITTLE BOOK OF RESTORATIVE JUSTICE FOR COLLEGES AND UNIVERSITIES, SECOND EDITION
Copyright © 2019 by Good Books, an imprint of Skyhorse Publishing, Inc.

All rights reserved. No part of this book may be reproduced in any manner without the express written consent of the publisher, except in the case of brief excerpts in critical reviews or articles. All inquiries should be addressed to Good Books, 307 West 36th Street, 11th Floor, New York, NY 10018.

Good Books books may be purchased in bulk at special discounts for sales promotion, corporate gifts, fund-raising, or educational purposes. Special editions can also be created to specifications. For details, contact the Special Sales Department, Good Books, 307 West 36th Street, 11th Floor, New York, NY 10018 or info@skyhorsepublishing.com.

Good Books is an imprint of Skyhorse Publishing, Inc.®, a Delaware corporation.

Visit our website at www.goodbooks.com.

10 9 8 7 6 5 4 3 2

Library of Congress Cataloging-in-Publication data is available on file.

ISBN: 978-1-68099-468-1
eBook ISBN: 978-1-68099-469-8

Printed in the United States of America

Table of Contents

Foreword

In *The Little Book of Restorative Justice for Colleges and Universities*, David Karp offers a succinct, comprehensive, and practical guide for implementing restorative practices in higher education. Although restorative justice has been used for campus-based student misconduct since the 1990s, there has been a surge of interest as colleges and universities are pushed into the public spotlight due to bias-motivated acts, sexual assaults, alcohol and drugs, and climate concerns about the learning environment. The time for a fresh and effective response is now as higher education struggles to act on Title IX regulations, greater campus diversity, and the limitations of judicial and legalistic processes for managing the growing complexity of campus issues.

Colleges and universities function as small cities or discrete communities. A campus-related event such as sexual assault by a prominent athlete, a student-organized protest against immigrant students, a fraternity social event that mocks African Americans, or the publicized felony of a faculty member has wide ripple effects that impact the entire campus. Moreover, seemingly separate jurisdictions such as residential life, student conduct, research ethics, staff performance, and administration policies and procedures intersect as part of a large and complex system. As Karp demonstrates, restorative justice is uniquely equipped to respond to the multiple needs of different constituencies and to the demands of overlapping jurisdictions. Indeed, the increasingly recognized need for restorative justice in higher education for both wrongdoing and prevention suggests that it is fast becoming a public health rather than just a criminal justice intervention.

Although campus life is marked by its intricacies, Karp applies restorative justice to fact situations in higher education with exquisite clarity such that his explanations and examples are understandable and readily transferable across institutions. He sets the stage for the book by telling a story about the theft of a fiberglass statue from an antique shop by a college student and his use of a restorative process, as a college administrator, to repair damage and restore community trust. He makes the case that within higher education, restorative justice not only provides a disciplinary response, but one that also advances a student's learning commensurate with that student's social development and the educational mission of the institution. This dual agenda is undergirded by the core principles of restorative justice, namely, inclusive decision making, active accountability, repairing harm, and rebuilding trust. Karp discusses the role of restorative justice in student codes of conduct. Although codes generally use a progressive model of exclusion for conduct cases that separate the student from the institution, the focus on harm in restorative justice necessitates a coming together for moral dialogue about the impact of persons' behaviors on others.

Karp reviews three practices used on campuses, namely, restorative justice conferences, circles, and boards, as well as commonly used measures for amends making and rebuilding trust such as apologies, restitution, and community service. Of particular note are Circles of Support and Accountability, a powerful practice that helps students reintegrate into the campus community after they have been suspended. Karp provides an illustration of a complex circle to show the variety of harms and multiple voices that can be part of a restorative response. He also includes research on the effectiveness of these practices with particular emphasis on participant satisfaction, recidivism, and student offender learning outcomes.

Campuses are increasingly concerned with incidents of bias and abuses of power and privilege. These concerns require a wider lens and focus on social justice and improving the campus climate. Karp provides guidelines for multipartial facilitation in support of community building and responding to varying degrees of social power. This wide-angled lens is also central to implementing restorative justice on college and university campuses because it challenges the status quo. Indeed, restorative justice takes time and can require a revamping of current operations in the context of limited resources. Besides a list of critical areas for consideration, Karp includes brief case studies from several universities that detail the steps taken to advance restorative justice on campus. Finally, Karp includes three chapters, facilitating a campus-based training, preparing for a restorative justice conference, and conducting a conference using a script. These chapters give guidance on selecting trainers and the training agenda, critical areas to address prior to bringing stakeholders together for dialogue, and a catalog of the specific steps a facilitator takes to guide a conference. Collectively, these chapters provide a hands-on "how-to" package that allows readers to move from abstract principles to concrete application. Karp concludes with a vignette about the impact of restorative justice on a criminal justice class when a classmate's off-campus house was burglarized.

Karp packs this little book with a truckload of information. He also grounds the chapters in restorative justice values while challenging readers to recognize that how they respond to student misconduct on campus symbolizes the kind of community they aspire to be. Most important, Karp demonstrates how to make complex situations manageable while also using them as opportunities for personal growth and campus-wide healing.

Marilyn Armour
Professor and director of the Institute
for Restorative Justice and Restorative Dialogue
at the University of Texas at Austin

Acknowledgments

Many individuals have helped develop restorative practices for colleges and universities, and I am especially grateful to the following for their leadership, creativity, and advice with this book: Duke Fisher, Jasmyn Story, Kim Sullivan, Robert Rico, Sonoo Thadenay, Deb Eerkes, Chris Loschiavo, Josh Bacon, Matt Gregory, Rick Shafer, Nancy Schertzing, Paul Osincup, Stacy Vander Velde, Kevin Mowers, Justine Darling, and Casey Sacks.

Thanks also to Jo Fisher, who, with a keen editorial eye, streamlined the prose and cleaned up grammatical messes. And to Howard Zehr, the Little Books of Justice & Peacebuilding series editor, not only for supporting this project, but for doing so much to spread the word about restorative justice across the planet.

1.
Introduction:
The Story of Spirit Horse

Horse rustling is not the kind of trouble typically caused by college students. But Skidmore College, where I taught for many years, is located in Saratoga Springs, a small city in upstate New York that is known for its high-society thoroughbred racetrack. The population triples in the summertime, and the downtown streets become as bustling and lively as Greenwich Village.

Several years ago, the Saratoga County Arts Council launched a project that decorated the town with life-size fiberglass horses painted by local artists. One of the more interesting horses, called Spirit Horse, appeared to be passing through the large plate-glass window of an antique shop. The statue, cut in half, stood regally on the sidewalk with its rear end inside the store on the other side of the glass. The horse had two glowing green eyes that lit up at night, adding to the spectral mystique.[1]

Late one night, a Skidmore student was returning from the nearby bars and decided he wanted Spirit Horse for his very own. He was able to wrench the front half from its pedestal on the main thoroughfare and was also easily observed by a taxi driver and other witnesses. Police

© Mark Lawson

Restorative justice (RJ) is a philosophical approach that embraces the reparation of harm, healing of trauma, reconciliation of interpersonal conflict, reduction of social inequality, and reintegration of people who have been marginalized and outcast. RJ embraces community empowerment and participation, multi-partial facilitation, active accountability, and social support. A central practice of restorative justice is a collaborative decision-making process that includes harmed parties, people who caused harm, and others to seek a resolution that includes:
(a) accepting and acknowledging responsibility for harmful behavior,
(b) repairing the harm caused to individuals and the community, and
(c) working to rebuild trust by showing understanding of the harm, addressing personal issues, and building positive social connections.

arrived while he was still sweaty and out of breath from hauling it to his second story walk-up.

Though this was a minor incident along the continuum of crimes, college administrators were not pleased to read the front page headline, "Skidmore Student is Charged in Theft of Decorative Horse." They were rightly concerned this would reinforce a community perception of their students as selfish, overprivileged, and a nuisance.

As a restorative facilitator for this case, I was able to host a restorative justice dialogue with the key stakeholders including the student, the artist, the antique shop owner who had paid for the horse, and the arts council director. As is typical of the process, we worked through the case as a campus disciplinary matter before it was handled in the criminal court. There, the student had been charged with third-degree grand larceny and possession of burglary tools—a wrench and pliers.

The beginning of a conference includes storytelling by the student and each of the harmed parties. The arts council director was surprised to learn, for example, that the student had worked for his hometown's arts council the summer before. With a mixture of remorse and embarrassment, the student revealed that one of his motives in taking the horse was his appreciation for the project and his desire to have a souvenir from it. He quickly added his recognition that this was not the best way to support the arts.

When the restorative justice participants heard from the artist, it was the student's turn to be surprised. The artist described how he had been alerted quite early in the morning after the crime and quickly went downtown to inspect the damage. Of course, he said, he was upset about the theft and damage to his artwork. However, what really concerned him were the two live wires that had been ripped from the glowing eyes and left exposed on the sidewalk. He wondered aloud what would have happened had he not been there to remove them. Soon the street would have been filled with toddlers and dog-walkers. "Had the student considered that?" he asked.

The storytelling in a restorative justice process is designed to explore the harm caused by an offense. In this case, there was property damage and loss, but also the risk created by the electrical wires, the community-wide disappointment and anger about vandalism to a public art display, and a spoiling of the reputation of the college.

Once harms are listed, the group works toward solutions that can repair the damage and restore community trust. An agreement was reached in this conference that met everyone's concerns. The student was to be responsible for:

- Restitution to the artist for costs associated with repairing and reinstalling the horse.
- Restitution to the storeowner based on the cost of sponsoring the horse and the time period the horse was not on display.
- Community service at the Saratoga County Arts Council.
- A daily inspection and cleaning of the repaired "Spirit Horse" for the duration of the exhibit.
- Writing a letter to students moving off campus about being responsible neighbors (to be included in the Skidmore Student Off-Campus Housing Guide).
- Undergoing an alcohol evaluation.
- Organizing an alcohol-free social event on campus.

Impressed by the agreement reached at Skidmore, the Saratoga district attorney negotiated a sentence called "Adjournment in Contemplation of Dismissal." This meant that the student would admit guilt, but as long as he complied with the restorative agreement and stayed out of trouble for six months, his conviction would be sealed, and he would have no permanent criminal record.

About this book

When I facilitated the Spirit Horse case, I was an assistant professor just learning about restorative justice and how it was being applied in criminal justice cases around the world. We decided to apply RJ principles in this case and discovered the benefits for the student, the harmed parties, and the wider community. Personally, I learned the value of putting an academic interest to the test in a real-world case.

Nearly twenty years later, as a faculty member at the University of San Diego, I have continued to examine the use of restorative justice on the college campus through research, teaching, facilitator training and practice, and program implementation. As a student affairs administrator, I became deeply committed to the concept and practice of restorative justice. I have experienced how it can work given the very real pressures among campus conduct administrators to manage high case loads, ensure fair treatment, minimize institutional liability, protect the campus community, boost morale in a division with high turnover, and help students learn from their mistakes without creating insurmountable obstacles to their future successes.

I wrote this book to encourage colleges and universities to seriously consider implementing restorative practices on their campuses. It is designed to provide an overview of RJ principles and practices, evidence of its effectiveness, and tips on implementation. I provide case examples from a variety of campuses already using RJ, from large public universities to small, private liberal arts colleges.

Having conducted numerous campus RJ trainings, I have seen the need for a short, accessible guide to the topic that can be used as a training manual or stand alone as an introduction for campus decision-makers. Faculty who teach restorative justice may use this as a supplemental text that engages students in a topic of great concern to them—how they may be treated if they get in trouble.

Currently, many people question the value of higher education, arguing that it is too expensive, that students are not learning well, and that they are improperly trained to enter the workforce. In the race to cut costs and expand vocational training, institutions often forget to nurture the campus community. The Native American restorative justice practitioner, Ada Pecos Melton, reminds us that "restorative principles refer to the mending process for renewal of damaged personal and communal relationships."[2]

The way we respond to student misconduct symbolizes the kind of community we aspire to be. Just as criminal justice officials have learned they cannot incarcerate their way out of the crime problem, campus conduct administrators know they cannot suspend their way out of their student conduct problems. Restorative justice offers a different approach that is educational for the student while also meeting the needs of the harmed parties and the institution.

2.
The Principles of Restorative Justice

The Spirit Horse case illustrates four principles that are central to restorative justice.

Inclusive decision making

Restorative justice places decision making in the hands of the people most closely involved in the incident. RJ practitioners provide support and facilitation.

Active accountability

Restorative justice makes accountability active. People who cause harm must take responsibility and make amends. They cannot sit back and be judged and sanctioned.

Repairing harm

Restorative justice focuses on reparation and healing to bring harmed parties up, not to drag those who caused harm down.

Rebuilding trust

Restorative justice rebuilds relationships so that people who cause harm can be trusted again and harmed parties can again feel safe.

Inclusive decision making

Inviting people who cause harm to voice their ideas about how to repair it and asking victims and affected community members to articulate the harms they experienced and what needs they have—inviting them all to play a central role in creating a sanctioning agreement—illustrate the first core principle in restorative justice: *inclusive decision making.*

Sitting in a circle with facilitators who help guide the conversation but who do not offer ideas or solutions of their own, the participants play new and very different roles in the decision-making process from what is common in other campus conduct and judicial processes.

Consider, for example, the roles they play in the criminal courtroom. Defendants have a place to sit, but it is their attorneys who speak for them. Crime victims have no place except as observers in the gallery. And for witnesses, even the observer role is denied.

The most dissonant role in the courtroom is that of defendants, seemingly disengaged at their own trials, with nothing to do and little understanding of the technical language that is being spoken, which is so decisive regarding their fates. In the restorative process, the student, the artist, the storeowner, and the arts director are not marginalized observers, but central actors in the drama of decision making.

On college and university campuses, the standard disciplinary process is typically offender-centric. Most often, a single conduct administrator will meet with the student, discuss the incident, and decide on the spot what the sanction will be. Sometimes a conduct board will listen to the facts as presented by the accused student and a complainant, but the board will send them to a waiting room while it privately deliberates about the sanctions. Accused students and harmed parties do not have a strong voice in this process.

Because the artist, storeowner, and arts director are not members of the campus community, it is not likely that they would have been invited to participate or even hear about the outcome of the Spirit Horse case. They would not have learned of the campus's concern about the incident, and they would not learn anything about the student that might offset the negative stereotypes promoted in the local newspaper. They would not have been able to share the varied ways in which they were impacted by the incident and what needs and concerns they had in its aftermath.

Active accountability

Second, restorative justice focuses on *active accountability*. People who cause harm must take active responsibility for their transgressions. Often, in our criminal justice or campus conduct proceedings, offenders are able to distance themselves emotionally and remain quite passive.[2] The archetypal image is a young man sinking down in his chair with his arms crossed against his chest and a baseball cap pulled low over his brow. It is as if his body were saying, "I'm not here. You can't reach me." Even if he has admitted responsibility, often he will say, "Yes, I did it. I didn't mean it. Just tell me what you want me to do so I can get out of here."

The storytelling process is a direct challenge to this passive position. It is much harder to ignore the artist, shopkeeper, and arts director who are sharing real experiences and emotions and seeking to make eye contact with the student, drawing him outside of himself and into a larger, communal understanding of the incident and its consequences.

> *"This process, which I will refer to here as earned redemption, requires a sanctioning approach that allows offenders to make amends to those they have harmed to earn their way back into the trust of the community."[1]*
>
> Gordon Bazemore
> Professor of Criminal Justice
> Florida Atlantic University

A restorative facilitator asks, "Now that we have identified the harms, what can you do to make things right?" This question signals the importance of their active participation. Even if the first answer is "I don't know" or "whatever you tell me to," the facilitator's role is to continue to invite participation by probing and eliciting ideas.

It is through this process that students come to own the restorative obligations as their own, with their ideas included and their spoken commitment. This not only increases the likelihood that they will follow through, but also that they will not reject the tasks as coercively imposed or arbitrary.

Repairing harm

A third core principle in restorative justice is the focus on *repairing harm*. Restorative justice is guided by the question "How can the victim and the community be restored?" Traditional or retributive justice is guided by one that asks, "How should the offender be punished?"

In a sense, both questions respond to the symbolism of Lady Justice holding her scales. The crime has thrown the scales out of balance, and Lady Justice must right them. But the intentions are quite different—one is for repair and is victim-centered; the other is toward punishment and is offender-centered. Retributive justice wants to know what the college will do *to* the student to match the harm he caused to Spirit Horse and the community. Restorative justice wants to know what the college will *ask* of the student to make things right.

> "Restorative dialogue... [is where] the problem rather than the person is put in the center of the circle."[3]
>
> John Braithwaite
> Law Professor, Australian National University
>
> Declan Roche
> Law Professor, London School of Economics

It may, in the end, be challenging or difficult or unpleasant for the student to make amends, but this suffering is not the goal and is avoided, if possible. Instead, the goal is to do what can be done to repair the damage and return the community to a state of well-being.

How can the student contribute to the restoration and upkeep of Spirit Horse? How can he support the arts council? How can he improve relations between off-campus students and their neighbors? How can he encourage other students to avoid binge drinking and the poor judgments that go along with it? It is these questions that led to restitution, community service, a new off-campus housing guide, and organizing an alcohol-free social event as reparative tasks.

Rebuilding trust

Beyond repairing harm, a final core principle is included in restorative justice. This is to *rebuild trust*. The offending behavior naturally generates mistrust and hesitation about the status and inclusion of the offender in the community. The simplest and most tempting response is banishment from the community: imprisonment in the criminal justice system and suspension from campus.

In restorative justice, we seek to rebuild relationships between distrusting parties not because it is a "touchy-feely" solution, but because it is necessary for a stable community and often for the well-being of the victim. Because an offender has abrogated community trust, it is part of their obligation to renew it. Because trust is not quickly regained, the process fosters dialogue and mutual understanding and then clearly articulates tasks and benchmarks that build confidence in the community as they are achieved.

In Saratoga, the harmed parties were naturally wary of the horse thief's behavior, and they questioned him closely about his drinking. To help restore their confidence in him, the student agreed to participate in an alcohol evaluation and follow any recommendations from it.

It was a notable moment during the Spirit Horse case when the arts council director invited the student to do community service in her agency. Rather than moving in the direction of suspension, the conferencing dialogue enabled her to see the student as a multidimensional person—flawed in some areas but having strengths in others. With this nuanced perception, she saw how he could make a genuine contribution to her public arts projects, repairing the harm but also building positive relationships in the community.

Grounding a disciplinary response in these four RJ principles helps support student development by teaching students how to take responsibility for their misbehavior actively and productively. While most colleges and universities provide their students with clear conduct policies, they rarely articulate their punishment philosophy. In the next chapter, we will examine how restorative principles can be incorporated into campus codes of conduct.

3.
Restorative Justice in the Model Student Conduct Code

A t the University of California-Santa Barbara, some students were entertaining themselves in their residence hall lounge by binge drinking and lighting their leg hairs on fire.[1] One of the students, "Steve" (a pseudonym), accidentally lit the upholstered arm of his chair on fire. While stamping it out, he got carried away and proceeded to demolish several pieces of furniture. The damage was estimated to be over $500, subjecting Steve to felony vandalism charges as well as campus disciplinary review.

Model conduct codes

Without knowing much about Steve, it is easy to ponder sanctions proportionate to the offense. We might, for example, place Steve on probation, ask him to pay restitution, and suspend him from the residence hall. Most conduct administrators write their disciplinary policies based on model codes of student conduct published by national leaders in the field such as Gary Pavela,[2] as well as Edward Stoner and John Lowery.[3] These model codes enumerate a typical list of potential sanctions: warning, probation, loss of privileges, fines, restitution, residence hall suspension, academic suspension, expulsion.

While these sanctions are commonplace, we rarely examine the underlying philosophy behind them. Notably, this is a model of *progressive exclusion*. As the offense becomes more severe, the strategy is to further separate the student from the institution. This makes perfect sense if the goal is simply to protect the campus community from further harm or risk, but most conduct administrators also have a goal of helping students learn from their mistakes. Indeed, the Council for the Advancement of Standards in Higher Education argues that "Student Conduct Programs in higher education must enhance overall educational experiences by incorporating student learning and development outcomes in their mission."[4]

"Student conduct officers are not employed to find new and more efficient ways to dismiss students. One of our primary roles—recognizing that dismissals are sometimes necessary—is to help students who commit disciplinary offenses make amends and stay enrolled. That goal requires keeping a fresh and open mind to creative educational strategies."[5]

Gary Pavela
Director of Academic Integrity, Syracuse University

Conduct processes as education

Learning in student conduct often comes in two forms. First, Steve could learn that his behavior was morally wrong because it was harmful to the community. Second, he could learn that membership in a community implies a social contract and there are costs to nonconformity. The first has to do with a *moral* actor, one who considers whether an act is right or wrong. It assumes Steve can feel the pangs of conscience. The second refers to a *rational* actor, one who calculates risk and reward, costs and benefits. A conduct process can address both, but an educational process should always begin with a moral dialogue.

> **An educational process should always begin with a moral dialogue.**

A discussion of harm is inherently a moral dialogue because it focuses on the impact of the behavior on others. We would call a person who simply does not care about others amoral. It is not unusual for students like Steve to have tunnel vision, focusing solely on themselves. Calling attention to the harm through restorative practices redirects their attention, eliciting empathy and conscience. Most often, students "get it," feel remorseful, and are then ready to take responsibility by trying to make amends.

This is the ideal outcome in a conduct case because all parties may be reassured that the student shares the same moral standards and only needs to be reminded of them. Steve participated in an RJ conference and learned about the impact of his actions on an understaffed maintenance crew, how he had betrayed the trust of a residential life staff member who had stood up for him in the past, and how he had disappointed and worried his mother about his drinking and his ability to successfully complete college.

Limits to restorative approaches

Unfortunately, restorative practices do not always work and are not meant to replace other approaches. Instead, they are meant to precede them with the hope that other approaches will not be necessary. Some people are simply too self-consumed to care about the impact of their behavior on others. Failing to appeal to their conscience, we must appeal to their rationality. "Even if you do not care about this rule and the consequences of your behavior on others, you should recognize the cost of your behavior on yourself."

Deterrence is the overarching philosophy here. Rational offenders are deterred from future misbehavior because they do not enjoy getting caught and suffering the penalty. They analyze the risk and the costs and decide that causing more offense is not worth the trouble. Deterrence-based sanctions may be effective, but the outcome is less ideal than with restorative sanctions because they do not cultivate moral engagement.

Without a moral foundation, the misconduct may return.

Without a moral foundation, if the incentives change, the misconduct may return.

If the offender is neither moral nor rational, we are in deeper trouble. Such offenders are immune to moral appeals and rational disincentives. Fortunately, there are not many such individuals. It is for this group that we must respond with incapacitation, coercively stopping them from further offending. On the college campus, this generally means suspension or dismissal—removing them from the community either temporarily or permanently.

A sanctioning pyramid

Although it is common to pit one type of sanction against another, the sanctioning pyramid[6] suggests they can be complementary. One can be used for moral dialogue, another to establish proper disincentives, and a third as a last resort.

Braithwaite's Sanctioning Pyramid

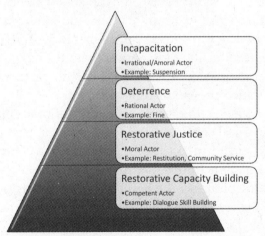

The pyramid encourages us to begin with a sanctioning approach that cultivates internal social controls or self-regulation. We treat students first as competent actors, capable of learning skills of interpersonal consideration, empathy, and conflict resolution. We want students to be guided by conscience, able to consider the long-term consequences of their actions for themselves and others. We also begin with restorative responses because this approach offers the most decision-making control to the core stakeholders. Harmed parties have a voice in the outcome. Offenders are more likely to take ownership because they are part of the decision.

People who cause harm are more likely to take ownership when they are part of the decision.

A misunderstanding of the sanctioning pyramid would be that RJ is best for minor violations and traditional punishments are best for serious ones. The severity of the violation is less important than its "significance" for the stakeholders. As long as the process is voluntary and the person who caused harm is willing to take responsibility, an RJ process can be used for the most serious campus harms. It is a process that may best meet all of the parties' needs in a situation they view as significant.

Consider the kinds of sanctions that emerged from Steve's RJ conference. He was asked to pay for the damage to the furniture and volunteer to work with the maintenance crew. Because of the group's concern about his alcohol use, he agreed to attend thirty Alcoholics Anonymous meetings. Because of his betrayal of trust with his resident assistant, the two agreed to work together on floor programming. Rather than distance Steve further from the campus community, these responses helped to strengthen his ties to the community by building positive relationships and strong mentoring opportunities.

While the sanctioning pyramid suggests that RJ and model conduct codes are complementary, it is important to distinguish them clearly.[7] Most important, traditional model code hearings are best used when accused students *deny responsibility*. Similar to the criminal court, model code hearings are carefully orchestrated to maintain civility, respectability, and fairness while board members listen to two opposing sides present evidence and counterevidence. Complainants, respondents,

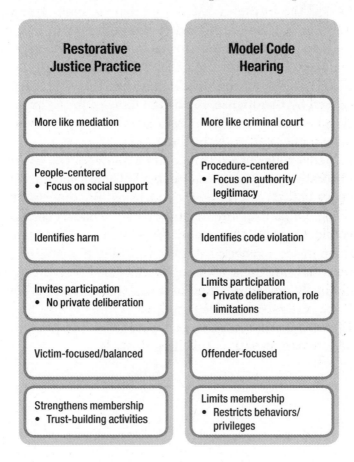

Restorative Justice Practice	Model Code Hearing
More like mediation	More like criminal court
People-centered • Focus on social support	Procedure-centered • Focus on authority/ legitimacy
Identifies harm	Identifies code violation
Invites participation • No private deliberation	Limits participation • Private deliberation, role limitations
Victim-focused/balanced	Offender-focused
Strengthens membership • Trust-building activities	Limits membership • Restricts behaviors/ privileges

witnesses, and advisors all have carefully prescribed roles. The primary goal is to determine if the accused student violated the student code of conduct, and board members undertake this in private deliberation. Sanctions, generally selected from a short menu of options, progressively limit membership from the campus community.

Restorative justice assumes that the accused student has admitted fault, which quickly shifts the focus toward the future—what can be done to make things right. Less attention is paid to procedures than to the participants and manifesting an authentic and engaged dialogue. The goals are to have the parties gain a deeper understanding of one another, acknowledge the harm caused by the offense, repair the damage to the extent possible, and strengthen the students' relationships with one another and with the institution.

Model codes of student conduct allow for the use of restorative sanctions because they include a general category called "discretionary sanctions" or "other sanctions." Of course, any institution can revise its code of conduct to highlight restorative options rather than hide them inside a generic category. In addition to outlining potential sanctions, codes of conduct also describe disciplinary procedures, and in the next chapter, I outline three restorative justice practices. While they all have RJ principles in common, each provides a different procedure or approach to fulfilling RJ goals.

4.
Three Models of Campus Practice

Restorative justice is a global movement with practices that have unique histories but borrow and blend as they evolve. Practices have emerged from contemporary criminal justice systems, faith-based communities, academia, and indigenous justice practices from Canada to New Zealand. The RJ pioneer, Dennis Maloney, once said, "Restorative justice is an ancient idea whose time has come."[1]

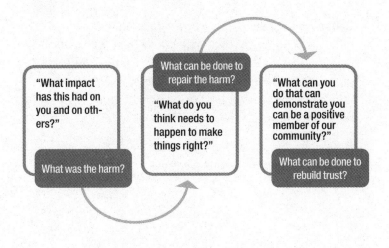

"What impact has this had on you and on others?"

What was the harm?

What can be done to repair the harm?

"What do you think needs to happen to make things right?"

"What can you do that can demonstrate you can be a positive member of our community?"

What can be done to rebuild trust?

As campuses begin to explore restorative justice, they borrow from various traditions and styles of practice. At the core of every practice, however, is a facilitated dialogue between offenders and harmed parties to identify the harm that was caused and how it can be repaired, including the goal of rebuilding trust.

While RJ practices share a common set of goals, three distinct practices are being implemented on college campuses: conferences, circles, and boards.

Restorative justice conferences

This model focuses on the facilitated dialogue between the offender and harmed parties. Also included are support people for both who help the parties feel more comfortable and capable of talking openly and honestly. After discussing the harm, the parties (instead of a hearing officer or conduct board) decide which steps the offender can take to repair the harm. Trained facilitators guide the dialogue.

> *"Conferencing is an opportunity for students who are referred to the conduct office to have a chance to meet face-to-face with the individuals they have impacted, take responsibility, make amends, build relationships, and move forward in a positive way through support from the campus community."[2]*
>
> Justine Darling
> Restorative Justice Coordinator
> University of San Diego

At the University of San Diego (USD), a Catholic university with more than 8,000 students, RJ conferencing began as collaboration between the Office of Student Conduct and the USD Joan B. Kroc School of Peace Studies. As the program grew, the conduct office changed its name to the Office of Ethical Development and Restorative Practices. RJ conferences are hosted by trained facilitators, who use a script to guide the flow of dialogue (see Chapter 12). Prior to the conference, the facilitator meets with the parties involved to educate them about the program and learn about the details of the case.

Like the University of San Diego, Michigan State University also uses restorative conferencing. The Department of Student Life at MSU handles conduct issues and once received a complaint that "Henry" had disrupted a final exam when he entered the classroom to retrieve a personal item, was asked to leave, and then became belligerent.[3] A conduct administrator met with Henry to explain the conduct process and decide if this would be a good case to refer to RJ. Hearing Henry admit to the misconduct, the conduct administrator suggested that he try the RJ process as an interim step before proceeding to a conduct hearing. If successful, the conduct hearing might no longer be necessary. When Henry agreed, the conduct administrator referred the case to the RJ facilitator.

Once the RJ facilitator receives a referral, the next step is to determine who should participate in the RJ conference. In this instance, harmed parties included the students who were taking the exam, the proctor who told Henry to leave the classroom, and the professor for the course. During the preconference meetings, the facilitator learned that the proctor wished to participate but would be unable to attend because she would be at an internship several hours away. The facilitator had to choose between excluding the proctor, having the proctor write an impact statement to be read at the conference, rescheduling, or having the proctor participate by phone or Skype. Working with the proctor, they decided that a telephone conference call would work best.

During the conference, Henry was able to take responsibility for his behavior and express his remorse. The harmed parties were able to share exactly how they were impacted. For example, they explained that a number of students submitted incomplete exams, stating that the disruptions had made it hard for them to finish on time. One student, who did finish on time, said it had been difficult to concentrate, and she didn't do as well as she could have. Afterward, the professor allowed students to complete a make-up exam, which was an extra burden for both the students and the faculty member.

Once the harms had been identified, the participants agreed to have Henry write a letter of apology to the students who had been taking the final exam. The faculty member would distribute the letter (without Henry's name because of confidentiality concerns), believing it was an important way to show that the department took action and held the student accountable. The faculty member also agreed to withdraw the complaint after the apology letter was received, so that a conduct hearing would not be necessary.

Soon after the conference, Henry submitted a draft of the apology letter to the facilitator, who used this as an opportunity to provide guidance and support and to make sure that the letter was well written and would be well received by the harmed parties. Students in the class let the faculty member know that they appreciated the letter. Because the case was handled informally, the student was able to avoid a conduct hearing and a permanent disciplinary record.

Restorative justice circles

RJ circles are similar to RJ conferences but often involve a larger number of people and borrow practices from indigenous traditions, especially the Native American practice of using a "talking piece." This is a symbolic or sacred object that is held by the speaker, encouraging honest, courageous sharing and signifies to those without the talking piece to listen for deeper understanding. The talking piece is passed around the circle, creating a unique rhythm of dialogue. At James Madison University in Virginia, a JMU centennial medallion is used because it symbolizes the values and culture of the institution—its one-hundred-year history and the pursuit of liberal learning. The talking piece becomes a reminder of their common values and purpose.

Circle practices may have a spiritual dimension to them, sometimes drawing directly on indigenous rituals and stories or the particular culture or faith of an institution. Christian schools, like Liberty University in Virginia, sometimes incorporate prayer into their circles. JMU, a secular public university, draws upon the "Madison Way," a set of eight principles that guides membership in the campus community: scholarly, honest, studious, accountable, respectful, resilient, compassionate, and invigorating. In addition to the talking piece, JMU includes a copy of the Madison Way as a centerpiece in the middle of the circle, and the facilitator or "circle keeper" talks about it as part of the introduction.

"At James Madison University, the restorative practice we use the most is the circle process. We have found the key to a successful restorative circle is the precircle work. This includes meetings with the harmed party, the party that caused the harm, community stakeholders, and cofacilitators. We use the circle process not only for issues where harm has been done, but to build community in various groups, organizations, and teams (including residence halls, athletic teams, fraternities and sororities, and leadership groups). Many people have commented at the end of a circle process how easy it was for the facilitator and how the facilitator barely did anything. This couldn't be further from the truth; the facilitator is responsible for the precircle work, introducing the process and the guidelines, and facilitating dialogue that respectfully addresses the harms, needs, and obligations of all circle participants. A good facilitator will be not only listening, but watching nonverbal communication in order to determine how to proceed."[4]

Josh Bacon
Dean of Students, James Madison University

Organizing a Circle in Four Rounds

The facilitator is responsible for setting a tone of respect, hope, and support. Circles tend to be organized in four "rounds," with the talking piece making its way around the circle at least once per round.

Round 1: Connection (Building Trust)

During the *first* introductory round, the facilitator welcomes the group and summarizes the issue that brought everyone together. Participants introduce themselves, explain why they are present, and express what they hope to achieve from the process. The facilitator summarizes the hopes expressed. Time is then taken to share stories that help the participants feel connected to one another and build trust.

Round 2: Concern (Exploring the Issue)

In the *second* round, participants share their feelings and perceptions about the topic of concern, identifying aspects that are important to them. The facilitator summarizes key emerging themes, areas of agreement and disagreement, and the harm that has been identified.

Round 3: Collaboration (Brainstorming Next Steps)

During the *third* round, participants share ideas about what needs to happen for resolution to occur. They explore how to address unmet needs and repair harm.

Round 4: Closing (Assessment and Appreciation)

Finally, the closing round enables participants to offer final comments or observations about what the circle meant to them.

In addition to conduct cases, circles are often used for disputes, such as fights where the line is blurred between who is an offender and who is a harmed party. Circles are also used for incidents where there is no offender or the offender has not been identified, but harmed parties want to share their concerns, find support, and/or create plans for the future.

A powerful example of using a circle process was at the University of Vermont after a student committed suicide. According to Residence Life Director Stacey Miller, "We couldn't have known when we started doing community circles that a tragedy like this would occur. . . . But since we were already doing the circles, when a crisis hit we knew exactly what to do. . . . The process has given our students a voice; a voice to share how they feel, heal, and move forward together."[5]

Restorative justice boards

Restorative justice boards have the structure of a "model code" conduct board with standing board members who may be drawn from faculty, staff, and students. However, they are run more like an RJ conference than a model code hearing. Harmed parties are invited but are not needed for the board to proceed. While RJ boards retain the ability to have private deliberations and make their own determinations about sanctions, these practices are avoided to increase the active participation of accused students and harmed parties.

The clear advantage of this model is that all conduct cases may be referred to the board, whereas other RJ practices are careful to limit RJ referrals to cases where a harmed party is willing to participate and a student admits to causing harm. When a harmed party declines, then board members will represent their perspective, often by reading an impact statement.

More broadly, board members serve as representatives of the community and speak to the harm caused indirectly, such as how the student may have tarnished the reputation of the institution. When the case is adversarial—the offender is denying responsibility—the board operates initially very similarly to a model code hearing by reviewing the evidence and making a determination. However, during the sanctioning portion of the board process, the decision making is focused on the key RJ goals of *repairing harm* and *rebuilding trust*.

While boards offer gains in efficiency, they do have some disadvantages. Some of the emotional immediacy of conferencing and circles is lost by having several participants (board members) who were not directly involved in the incident. Without a direct connection, board members can start to treat cases in a routine or formulaic manner, almost jaded by the repetition of similar cases. Finally, because boards can proceed without harmed parties, they may become complacent about recruiting their participation.

The models compared

Because most campuses rely on one-on-one administrative hearings to manage their caseloads, many have incorporated restorative practices into their hearings. Typically, this would include an emphasis on identifying what harm was caused by the offense and how the student can repair it. But it can also include inviting harmed parties to participate in the hearing, essentially transforming the hearing into an RJ conference.

Deciding which practice is best for a campus depends on the goals of the initiative. Boards are often the easiest to implement because most campuses already have conduct boards in place, and they can be modified to employ RJ principles. Conferencing can be used for a select group of RJ cases, either because the parties involved are very amenable to the process or because the incident has garnered a lot of campus attention and requires careful handling. Circle practices are especially powerful because their structured dialogue enables every person to have an equal voice in the process. They may also have a particularly spiritual quality to them and are often adopted by faith-based institutions.

	Conferencing	Circles	Boards
Participants	• Facilitators • Offender • Harmed parties • Support persons	• Circle keepers • Offender • Harmed parties • Support persons	• Board chair and members • Offender • Harmed parties • Support persons
Process	• Structured and unstructured dialogue	• Circle process with talking piece	• Structured and unstructured dialogue
Niche	• Featuring harmed parties • Opportunity to train pool of volunteer facilitators (students, faculty, staff)	• Including large numbers of harmed parties • Resolving mixed-responsibility conflicts • Cases with unknown offenders • Featuring campus cultural symbols and rituals	• "Victimless" and quality of life offenses • Community in general can be the harmed party • Cases when harmed parties decline participation • Easy to implement/ transition from traditional conduct board • Can include determination of responsibility
Examples	• Theft, harassment, assault, academic integrity	• Fights, roommate conflicts, bias incidents, noise	• Underage drinking, disorderly conduct, DWI, weapons possession
Tradition	• Mennonite victim-offender reconciliation programs, victim-offender mediation, and New Zealand Maori justice	• Justice practices of Native American and Canadian First Nation peoples	• Vermont Community Reparative Boards (Probation) and South African Truth and Reconciliation Commission

Perhaps the biggest contrast between traditional conduct hearings and restorative practices is the emphasis that RJ places on identifying and repairing harm. While traditional practices focus on whether or not the student violated the conduct code, often carefully parsing which specific policy was violated, RJ dialogues explore the nature of the harm. The next chapter provides one method for this examination.

5.
Identifying Harms and Needs

Storytelling is central to restorative justice because it allows people to tell their story of harm (whether they experienced harm or caused it). Facilitators ask questions that allow for storytelling, but they are primarily listening for harms and any needs people might have as a result of them. They might include harms that fall into the following four categories:

Types of Harm

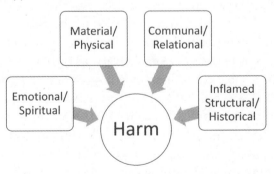

At a Texas university, the president of a fraternity, "William" (a pseudonym), and several of his brothers were in a private group chat conversation about the World Cup soccer tournament, which then turned to issues concerning illegal immigration. William suggested legalizing the shooting of immigrants who crossed the border. "I'm telling you build a wall, and the us govt. can sell permits for legal hunting on the border and we can make a sport of this, can be a new tax revenue stream for the govt." His comments were made public and received local and national news attention. The campus and the broader community were harmed and outraged, demanding that the university take strong disciplinary action.

While university senior administrators explored the possibility of expulsion, they were advised by legal counsel that William's comments were protected free speech. Because of the community outrage, William voluntarily resigned his position as fraternity president, but the campus community remained dissatisfied by their perceived administrative inaction.

The university administration wanted the needs of the harmed parties to be addressed. Since traditional student conduct sanctions were not an option, they hired two experienced restorative practitioners, Robert Rico and Kim Sullivan, to facilitate the process. The facilitators met with William first, partly to assess his willingness to take responsibility and to ensure his participation was voluntary. William expressed genuine remorse for what he had said and that what he most wanted to do was to make it right. He also described how difficult life had been since the incident—losing a prominent role on campus that kept him highly engaged; losing many friends; being rejected from a job opportunity; and feeling lonely, isolated, and ashamed.

Next, the facilitators met with different representatives from harmed student groups including the president of

the student government and other multicultural fraternity and sorority presidents. They described a variety
of harms. Many were angry, scared, and hurt following
the incident, all indicators of *emotional/spiritual harm*.
Some were displeased with the administration's lack
of action and problems with communication. They did
not believe the administration had conducted effective outreach to ensure their full participation. These
reflected *communal/relational harms*. The need for the
university to spend time and resources on this incident
is an example of *physical/material harm*.

The restorative justice circle lasted several hours. A
Latinx student shared that on the night the comments
went viral, she had a nightmare that her entire family
was murdered in front of her. Students of color shared
that they were scared to be around white people and that
this incident heightened their fears. They worried about
what people were thinking of them and were on guard
for incidents of bias and racism. Other harmed students
shared that, sadly, they were not surprised by the incident and felt that the university has underlying issues
with racism and inclusivity. Some mentioned visual rep-
resentations on campus with a lack of diversity in art
and decoration. All of these harms are associated with
inflamed structural/historical harm, demonstrating how
even a private comment, not intentionally directed at the
harmed parties, can trigger profound reactions because
of the comment's association with the contemporary
political climate and a history of racism.

William expressed his apology and regret for his
statements and said he was willing to do anything
they suggested to make things right. The facilitators
sensed genuine remorse and sadness about the impact

his comments had on others. He mentioned that since the incident, he felt that he had no sense of purpose or direction. He commented at the end of the circle that he finally felt "useful" again. He wanted to make amends.

A reparation plan to address the harms was collaboratively constructed. William would:

- Meet with any groups interested in hosting him at a chapter meeting or event.
- Assist other group leaders in gaining access to higher levels of the administration.
- Volunteer at a Latinx nonprofit.
- Connect student leaders with the Inter-Fraternity Council and organize a meeting about diversity and inclusion.
- Attend and support Multicultural Greek Council events and show support by reaching out to leaders and following their Instagram accounts.
- Audit (for the remainder of the semester) a class geared toward social justice, diversity, and ethics.

Some of the broader community needs agreed upon during the reparation plan were:

- Bridge a perceived divide among the Greek Councils.
- Request a circle process with key administrators to address concerns with the administration.
- Consider how the administration can address issues of accountability and follow-up for any future bias incidents.
- Enlist others at all levels (e.g., faculty and staff) to create a more inclusive community.
- Create more opportunities for diverse student voices to be heard and considered when making community decisions.

"The restorative justice joint circle ended up being an incredible experience with many groups represented and true understanding achieved between William and the harmed parties. It created a space for students to share not only about the incident, but also about larger systemic concerns with the administration and campus community. The circle process created a safe space for all participants to speak and listen from the heart. It planted a seed to continue discussions about the disconnectedness of the campus community and to foster healthy relationships."

Robert Rico, MPA
Lecturer, Department of Criminal Justice
University of Texas at San Antonio

Kim Sullivan, JD
Director, Conflict Management and Dispute Resolution Office
University of Texas at Austin

Many conduct administrators believe that consistency is important: similar violations should lead to similar sanctions. In restorative justice, sanctions are tailored to the needs and concerns of the circle participants as they are identified in the storytelling process. This approach recognizes the complexities of each incident. Two may be identical in how they are listed as conduct violations (or as protected free speech) but quite different in the harms caused, the attitude and risk level of the offender, and the will of the group for the best response to the situation.

The process of identifying harm is important because it helps the offender to understand the consequences of their behavior and allows the participants to specifically address them in the agreement. The next chapter provides suggestions about how to make RJ sanctions as successful as possible.

6.
Best Practices in Repairing Harm and Rebuilding Trust

Rupert Ross, a Canadian attorney and prosecutor, has written about his experience with restorative justice in First Nations communities. He observed, "An offender cannot even *know* what he did until he begins to learn, first-hand and in a feeling way, how people were affected by it."[1]

The first question we ask in a restorative process helps us to acknowledge that harm has taken place. A restorative dialogue explores the nature of this harm. This is why it is so important to include people who were impacted by the offense. By including harmed parties, offenders have a chance to learn about the actual harm caused by their behavior.

Once the harm is identified, the participants can explore how the harm can be repaired. Solutions often include a combination of tasks that respond to four kinds of harm: emotional/spiritual harm, material/physical harm, relational/communal harm, and inflamed structural/historical harm. Dialogue and apology are a response to emotional harm. Repair, restitution, and support for recovery address material or physical harm. Community service mends the social fabric, while supportive reintegration responds to community concerns. Social justice engagement and a focus on policy change begins the process of healing inflamed structural/historical harm. Restorative justice does not presume that harms can be fully repaired or that those who caused it have the capacity to do so individually or even with community support. The goal is to engage in a restorative process that recognizes the significance of the harm with proportionate commitment and obligation.

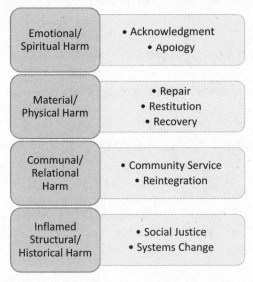

Emotional/ Spiritual Harm	• Acknowledgment • Apology
Material/ Physical Harm	• Repair • Restitution • Recovery
Communal/ Relational Harm	• Community Service • Reintegration
Inflamed Structural/ Historical Harm	• Social Justice • Systems Change

Apology guidelines

"An apology is a good way to have the last word."
Author unknown

Apologies are expressions of remorse and the willingness to take responsibility for a transgression. They must be sincere if they are to be taken seriously. Apologies are an important way to repair community relationships and restore trust between parties. When apologies are included in restorative agreements, they should be written (not verbal) and approved before sending to a harmed party.

Apology letters should include:

What happened
- A description detailing the harm caused by the offense. This shows that the person understands the harmful consequences of their behavior.

My role
- An acknowledgment of responsibility for the offense. Watch out for expressions that deny, displace, or minimize responsibility.

How I feel
- An expression of remorse or regret for causing harm.

What I won't do
- A commitment to responsible behavior and steps that will be taken to reduce the chance of reoffending.

What I will do
- An outline of how needs will be met and amends will be made for the harm caused.

Students often spontaneously provide verbal apologies during RJ conferences, and these are important moments in the dialogue. It is not expected that they will capture all of the elements of the written apology guidelines. The same is true for first drafts. Mentoring a student through the apology-writing process is a tremendous student development opportunity.

Restitution guidelines

Restitution is monetary payment or labor that pays for financial losses. Labor can be defined broadly to include creative projects or symbolic activities such as an art student who pays restitution to the harmed party by painting her portrait. Restitution is very different from fines, even though they can both involve money. Fines are a punitive sanction meant to impose a cost or burden upon the offender and usually go to the institution. The amount is determined by what is believed to be effective in deterring repeat offending. Restitution is determined by an accounting of the losses incurred by the harmed party and goes to the harmed party.

Restitution agreements should include:

Monetary losses
- Clear specification of financial or property losses to the harmed party.

Payment plan
- A payment plan that meets the needs of the harmed party but also takes into account the person's ability to pay.
- Sometimes labor or other creative endeavors are substituted for payment.

Community service guidelines

Volunteering in the community is a way to be helpful to others, show that one is socially responsible, and rebuild the trust that is lost through misbehavior. Community service should be meaningful and rewarding. Community service can meet several goals:

- Making amends to the community.
- Demonstrating good citizenship.
- Developing new relationships with positive peers and mentors.
- Educating the community about the RJ process.

Community service projects should include:

Proposal
- Students should take the lead on proposing a relevant form of community service. Proposals should include:
  - The type of service project.
  - How the service makes amends for harm done to the community.
  - Learning goals for the student's personal development.
  - A timeline for service completion.

Validation
- A letter, signed by a service agency staff member, to verify that the project was completed satisfactorily.

Reflection
- A letter describing the value of service experience personally and for the community.

Consider, for example, two roommates who took lounge furniture into their room while also leaving the common area a mess. A turning point in their RJ conference happened when another student, who worked as a tour guide, described how embarrassing it was to show the residence hall to prospective students in the condition they had left it. In response, the roommates recognized an important harm and proposed organizing a dorm-wide "spring cleaning" in preparation for a major admissions event. This kind of community service helped repair the harm they had caused while also providing the offenders a way to be positive leaders on campus.

Social Justice Engagement Guidelines

According to RJ facilitator Jasmyn Story,[2] inflamed structural/historical harm evokes or alludes to traumatizing structural or historical violence. The original structural or historical harm may span generations of communities, leaving a legacy of group trauma.[3] By acknowledging and responding to this harm, the responsible party has an opportunity to help shift the conditions in which they were created or sustained. Restorative responses to structural/historical harm are often collaborative efforts informed by the harmed community in order to advocate for change. Although a restorative response to one individual incident is unlikely to bring significant social change, it provides the opportunity to highlight the deeper issues and focus efforts not only on reparation, but also on community education and policy change.

Social justice engagement should include:
- Deep understanding of the legacy of harm, inflamed by the incident, and its intersectional implications.
- Analysis of how the harm is manifested in the local, directly impacted community.

- A commitment to addressing the legacy or the current iteration of the structural/historical harm.

Advocacy and engagement projects should be:
- Informed by the needs and concerns of the harmed parties/impacted community.
- Considerate of the narratives of harmed parties, which would be shared only with their consent.
- Constructed thoughtfully with a proposal, a form of validation, and a reflective component (like community service projects).

Trust-building activities

In addition to repairing harm, when a student commits a violation, it is natural and appropriate for the campus community to question their trustworthiness. A restorative dialogue helps the participants come to understand why the person chose to engage in the misbehavior. It helps to identify positive actions that they could undertake that will help reassure everyone that the behavior will not be repeated. An RJ dialogue is focused on how the student can demonstrate responsibility and learn to be a trustworthy member of the campus community.

Separation may be an outcome when the RJ process cannot identify a viable strategy for reassurance. RJ participants are concerned with the question "What will reassure us that you

Separation may be an outcome when RJ cannot identify a viable alternative for reassurance.

will be a positive member of the campus community?" Often, such reassurance occurs when the student commits to involvements that reduce the likelihood that they will reoffend. These involvements can include: seeking counseling or other help that reduces personal risk factors; activities that show how they can be positive and invested members of the community, like running for a leadership position; and/or activities that help them further explore and understand the harm they caused, such as a research project about the issue and organizing a campus program to educate other students about it.

A stronger practice for reassuring the community is to create Circles of Support and Accountability (CoSA). Given the recent focus on campus sexual misconduct, students are being held more accountable, and suspensions are on the rise. CoSA is a highly successful model that was created for high-risk sex offenders returning to the community from prison. A trained group of volunteers meet with the offender on a regular basis to offer support during their transition as well as monitoring. A similar model can be used for students reintegrating into the campus community from suspension for sexual and gender-based misconduct, alcohol or drug abuse, or any other violation where the community may be nervous about the student's return.[4]

An example of trust building

A highly intoxicated University of Florida student, "Derek," confronted his ex-girlfriend about their breakup. As they argued, he got into her car and refused to leave. So she drove to the campus police station, where Derek had to be physically removed by several officers. A restorative justice conference was convened, and the participants debated whether or not Derek should be able to return to the institution. Although it helped that he was very remorseful and had no prior disciplinary record, the participants, particularly four law enforcement officers, really needed to be persuaded. To do this, Derek agreed that he would seek counseling to address anger, relationship, and substance abuse issues. In addition, he agreed to collaborate with the police officers to present a campus workshop on the legal ramifications of alcohol and drug use.

"Law enforcement often refers cases to student conduct and then never hears an outcome or doesn't understand why a student is still on campus or has returned to campus. In this case, RJ allowed for law enforcement to have a say in the outcome and provided them with a better understanding of the student besides what they saw at the time of the incident."[5]

Chris Loschiavo
Director of Student Conduct and Conflict Resolution
University of Florida

RJ does not rely simply on a student's promise to be good; in this case, it was his active role in seeking counseling and a service project that strengthened his ties to campus police while showing a positive leadership role that rebuilt community trust.

Just as it is important for a student to demonstrate their reliability, it is important to determine if RJ is as effective in meeting its goals. The next chapter reviews recent research on the use of RJ in campus conduct.

7.
Does It Work?
Research and Assessment
of Campus Restorative
Programs

Hundreds of empirical studies have been conducted measuring the effectiveness of restorative justice in criminal justice, K–12, and higher education settings.[1]

To explore the effectiveness of campus restorative justice, I conducted a study called the STARR Project (STudent Accountability and Restorative Research Project).[2] The research team gathered data on 659 conduct cases from eighteen schools throughout the United States, including large public institutions and liberal arts colleges, both secular and faith-based. We compared restorative practices with traditional model code hearings.

Appeals, completion, and reoffending

RJ and model code hearings tend to produce similarly low numbers of appeals, high rates of program completion, and relatively few repeat offenders. Appeals were rare overall, but practically nonexistent in RJ cases (less than one percent). This was less than in model code cases, which had an appeal rate of 4 percent. Both practices had similarly high rates of compliance, with 93 percent of students completing their sanctions within one year of the hearing. And both practices had similar rates of reoffending, about 18 percent within one year. However, when students reoffended after an RJ intervention, their violations tended to be less serious than model code reoffenders.

Participant satisfaction

In the STARR Project, RJ practices sharply contrasted with model code hearings by their inclusion of harmed parties in the dialogue process. The table below shows

Harmed Party Satisfaction With Restorative Justice Process

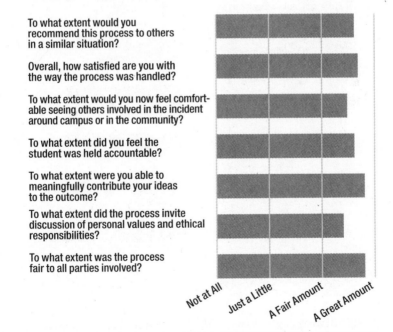

that harmed parties consistently and strongly appreciated this opportunity for participation.[3]

Student learning

Student affairs professionals are *educators* and recognize that when students get in trouble, there is opportunity to use the conduct process to teach them important life lessons about the responsibilities of community membership. In the STARR Project, we explored six dimensions of student learning and found that restorative practices created an excellent opportunity for learning.[4] In each case, RJ yielded statistically significant improvements in learning over model code hearings.

Student Learning Outcomes

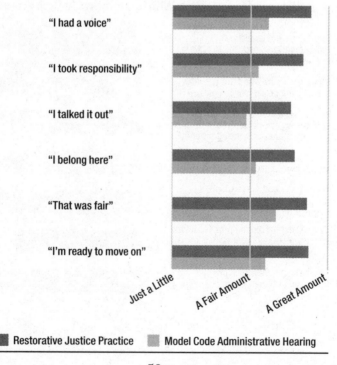

"I had a voice"

"I took responsibility"

"I talked it out"

"I belong here"

"That was fair"

"I'm ready to move on"

Just a Little   A Fair Amount   A Great Amount

■ Restorative Justice Practice   ■ Model Code Administrative Hearing

The categories of student development

"I had a voice" refers to the active participation of the student in the decision-making process. It has the student development goal of internalizing community standards so behavior is guided by conscience and recognition of the ethical responsibilities inherent in community membership.

"I took responsibility" refers to how much students understand not only that the behavior was a violation of rules, but also the consequences of the behavior for others, and their willingness to take responsibility for making things right.

"I talked it out" refers to the ability to listen to others' perspectives, express remorse, and repair fractured relationships at least to the point that students in conflict can safely and civilly coexist in the campus community.

"I belong here" refers to the student's social ties to the campus community, including a positive, nonadversarial orientation to campus administrators and police.

"That was fair" refers to the belief that the conduct process was fair, which helps create a sense of legitimacy for the rules and standards of the institution.

"I'm ready to move on" refers to satisfaction with the process leading to closure: facing up to the misconduct, learning from it, but not letting it become an obstacle to future success.

Overall, these findings are very encouraging. They suggest that it is possible to effectively respond to the needs of harmed parties while holding students accountable in a way that enhances student learning and development. Participants believe the process is fair and that this was a meaningful way to hold the people accountable for their misbehavior.

8.
Restorative Justice and Social Justice

College campuses are using restorative practices to respond to larger social justice issues such as sexual misconduct,[1] abuses of power and privilege,[2] and bias incidents.[3] For example, the University of California Office of the President has recommended that each of its ten campuses explore the use of RJ "when dealing with incidents of intolerance or hate, particularly for conduct that, while offensive, may not violate any laws or policies."[4] Any thoughtful restorative justice process should simultaneously address the needs and obligations of the key stakeholders and also consider the systemic reasons that allowed for the harm to take place.

At Colorado State University (CSU), two floormates in a residence hall got along poorly, and one of them, "Keith," called the other a "Chink." Later, in the dining hall, the harmed party, who was Asian, responded by loudly yelling, "This is the reason that stuff like Virginia Tech happens!"—referring to the 2007 incident when a student, Seung-Hui Cho, shot and killed thirty-two people and wounded seventeen others. CSU's restorative justice program held a restorative conference that included, among others, Keith, his coach who served as his support person, the harmed party, and the harmed party's support person.

The conference enabled the participants to speak openly about several important issues and come up with a restorative agreement that best addressed their concerns. The harmed party was able to communicate that the name-calling was offensive to him and caused him to feel marginalized during an already difficult transition to college. Keith acknowledged this, apologized, and shared his own challenges in making the transition. His coach helped Keith realize that some students have built-in support networks, such as a team, while others face more of a challenge finding their place in a large and often impersonal university. The harmed party was able to share that his outburst about Virginia Tech was not meant to be a threat and was able to reassure the participants that he did not intend to hurt anyone.

"I just don't think there is an educational workshop or other sanction that can duplicate sitting in front of the person you harmed and hearing how it affected them. I believe it is actually much more difficult to do this than simply showing up to a workshop."[5]

Paul Osincup
Associate Director of Conflict Resolution and
Conduct Services, Colorado State University

The conference created an agreement with several elements. Keith agreed not only to behave positively toward the harmed party, but that he would do what he could to ensure no one else on their floor would feel bullied for the rest of their year together. The coach offered to take the harmed party to watch a practice or game as a strategy to help him feel less isolated and to build a positive relationship with Keith. The harmed party formed a plan to meet with the director of the Asian/Pacific American Cultural Center, also as a strategy for him to find community at CSU.

Restorative justice is used as a strategy for community building and improving campus climate. Cases like this one help remind us that participants in any restorative process come from different backgrounds with varying degrees of social power. As a facilitator, it is vital to pay attention to social inequalities and try to offset power imbalances. RJ facilitators are not neutral or impartial, descriptions that might imply that we are indifferent, objective, disengaged, unemotional, or value-free. Instead, we are "multipartial," actively supporting all participants without preference or taking sides. In addition, facilitators must also be conscious of their own biases and influence. According to RJ scholar Marilyn Armour, "Even when we do not feel powerful, having more power creates the obligation to be aware of our impact."[6]

Typical power imbalances

- ≠ Offenders/harmed parties (sometimes harmed parties are afraid to speak to offenders)
- ≠ Harmed parties/offenders (sometimes offenders are overcome by shame)
- ≠ Facilitators/participants (facilitators can subconsciously steer the dialogue)
- ≠ Faculty/staff/students (students may be deferential to faculty or staff)

≠ Key stakeholders/less affected participants (less affected parties may not believe their needs are as important as those of others)

≠ Social identities (race, class, gender, sexuality, ability, religion, etc.)

≠ Group size (ratio of participants on offender's side/victim's side can affect how well participants feel supported)

Three of the more explicit expressions of power are (1) coalition-building—persuading other participants to accept one point of view, (2) air time—dominating the discussion, interrupting, not listening, and (3) inflexibility—stubborn refusal to move from stated position.

Multipartial facilitation techniques

= Keep social power in your awareness: assess the group and anticipate expressions of power.

= Cofacilitate with someone of a different social identity.

= Balance airtime: invite quiet members to share; use the circle process with a talking piece.

= First person narratives: invite "I statements" and personal sharing; discourage judgmental claims and attributions.

= Create space for quiet reflection: enable participants to gather their thoughts before speaking.

= Be encouraging: notice body language and facial expressions of raw emotion such as shame, sadness, or hopelessness and help participants see the opportunity the dialogue is providing to help meet needs and find resolution.

= Model authenticity and vulnerability: share relevant stories (but do not shift the focus from participants to the facilitator).
= Bring power dynamics to the surface: identify out loud what you are observing. Ask for clarification. Take the lead. Don't rely on less powerful individuals to challenge oppressive statements.
= Promise only what is realistic. Multipartial facilitation doesn't eliminate power differentials during or after the RJ dialogue. Facilitators often say an RJ circle is a "safe space," but it may not be (sometimes, they will say it is a "brave space" instead).
= Encourage respectful confidentiality, which helps provide some reassurance to otherwise marginalized voices: "What is said in the circle stays in the circle; what is learned in the circle leaves the circle."

9.
A Whole-Campus Approach to Implementation

Launching a new program can be a daunting process, especially in times of shrinking campus resources. Most conduct administrators complain that they are overburdened with cases, backlogged with email messages, and can never predict which day will bring a new student crisis. Building any new program is certainly time-consuming, and many would argue that RJ cases are more time-consuming than traditional administrative hearings. But it is also possible to refocus staff energy from hearing cases to training and managing RJ volunteers, a new and very empowering role that might increase morale and staff retention.

Borrowing from a model of RJ implementation in K–12 schools,[1] a whole-campus approach to restorative justice includes three tiers of activity. The first tier refers to restorative circles that are designed to build and strengthen community relationships. For example, many offices of residential life train their resident assistants to facilitate circles on their floors. The second tier includes restorative responses to individual incidents of conflict or harm. Circle practices are sometimes used to address widespread harm, such as when an incident causes a whole community to be on edge. Restorative conferences are typically used in cases that involve a discrete number of key stakeholders. The third tier focuses on reintegration after a period of separation. Circles of Support and Accountability can be used to assist with the transition of a student back to the campus community after a period of suspension.[2] The goal is to simultaneously help the student be successful while also reassuring the community that they will be responsible.

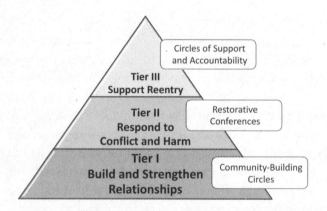

Perhaps the most important step toward implementation is to form an RJ working group and create a strategic plan. The working group might consider the following list and decide where their campus should begin implementing restorative practices:

- Conduct violations such as:
  - Bias incidents
  - Alcohol and drugs

- Sexual and gender-based misconduct
- Academic dishonesty
- Campus climate issues (nonviolation, e.g., free, but harmful, speech)
- Residential life/community building
- Off-campus housing/town-gown issues
- Athletics (team conflicts, violations, community building)
- Greek organizations
- Other student organizations
- Service learning opportunities in K–12 schools and criminal justice RJ
- Graduate student/post-doc issues
- Reentry support (conduct, medical/mental health, other types of leave)
- Workplace issues (faculty and staff conflicts or violations)
- Campus/city court partnerships
- Restorative coaching/mentoring

In addition to offering a few questions below that help bring focus to the implementation process, I have asked for insights about implementation from two esteemed colleagues who introduced restorative justice to their campuses.

Questions About Implementation

- What kind of restorative justice process resonates best with your campus culture or with the kinds of cases on which your program will focus? Conferencing, circles, boards?
- In which ways can you infuse RJ principles into current conduct practices and procedures?

- Which opportunities or constraints currently exist in your code of conduct for implementing an RJ program?
- Where do you need to foster support for the program? Student affairs administrators, legal counsel, campus safety, student government?
- Where will the program be housed? Conduct office, residential life, conflict resolution program?
- Do you have the right staff for a restorative justice program? Who will coordinate the program? Could the coordinating responsibilities be added to a current position?
- Who will facilitate cases—staff, faculty, graduate students, undergraduates?
- How much will a program cost? Which costs do you need to consider? Do you have financial support? How will you pay for the program?
- Can you connect/collaborate with a local restorative justice program? Are there possible partnerships with faculty or academic departments (higher education management, law, criminal justice, conflict analysis, peace studies, social work, etc.)? Which other resources can you utilize?
- How will you launch and market the program?
- What will be your referral streams? How can referrals be promoted?
- How would you implement training for the program? Who needs to receive training?
- How will you assess the effectiveness of your RJ program?

◇◇◇◇◇◇◇◇◇◇◇◇◇◇◇◇◇◇◇◇◇◇◇◇◇◇◇◇◇◇◇◇◇◇◇

Sonoo Thadaney Israni
Restorative Justice Pilot Program Manager
Stanford University

Many campuses, keen to explore restorative justice programs, frequently ask facilitators of Stanford's RJ pilot, "How did you get started?" Our Vice Provost of Student Affairs and Associate Vice Provost/Dean of Student Life have been interested in exploring alternative dispute resolutions to address student conduct issues. Peer mediation and restorative justice were priorities. Fortunately, we have also had support from alumni who are practitioners in the field and have supported us with their wisdom and funding.

Steps that launched Stanford's RJ pilot
1. Received leadership support from our Associate Vice Provost/Dean of Student Life and John Krumboltz, Professor of Education and Psychology, who teaches a course, cross-listed in both Education and Psychology, titled Mediation for Dispute Resolution.
2. Received funding and support from alumni, donors, and foundation.
3. Hired experienced RJ practitioner as program manager (25 percent FTE).
4. Researched existing RJ programs and shared with campus partners and leadership for feedback and customization.
5. Program manager attended two-day campus RJ training.

6. Developed program manual ensuring its alignment with existing mandates, protocols, and processes.
7. Customized assessment forms for respondents, harmed parties, facilitators, and observers.
8. Recruited volunteer facilitators including students and colleagues with experience in RJ and mediation and provided program orientation and facilitator training.
9. Scheduled a standard biweekly meeting time for case facilitation, case debriefing, and ongoing training. We found evenings to be most convenient and offered simple meals to build community and show appreciation.

◇◇◇◇◇◇◇◇◇◇◇◇◇◇◇◇◇◇◇◇◇◇◇◇◇◇◇◇◇◇◇

Deborah Eerkes
Director, Office of Student Judicial Affairs
University of Alberta

Prior to implementing our RJ program, the University of Alberta Residence Community Standards formed a cumbersome document, containing variations on the student conduct theme for each of the different residence halls. Eventually, the policy became too unwieldy to maintain, and the committee with primary oversight for student conduct policies demanded change.

Using all of the existing structures but replacing the underlying punitive principles with restorative ones, a new policy was drafted. Existing positions were retooled (for example, a student conduct administrator became a restorative agreement administrator), and conduct hearings were converted to restorative team meetings.

What followed was a marathon of consultation meetings sponsored by the Dean of Students with various campus stakeholders. Shifting the mindset from punitive to restorative proved challenging, and it became clear that reassurances were necessary. As part of the transition plan, we engaged local and international experts to assist in the training and rollout of the program who were committed to reviewing the program after each of the first and second years. With those assurances in place, the Board of Governors approved the new Residence Community Standards.

Residence Life and Judicial Affairs staff spent the summer designing training sessions, compiling manuals and other resources, and promoting the new program among staff and students. New staff was recruited using the updated job descriptions, and after training by both local and external RJ practitioners, the program went into effect.

Top five lessons learned at the University of Alberta
1. It was critical to have the support of the Provost and the Dean of Students before bringing an RJ program forward to the community for approval.
2. It was easier to adapt RJ to fit into our culture than to change our culture to accommodate RJ. The beauty of RJ is that it adapts to any environment and by its very nature changes a culture over time.
3. We needed to carefully answer the policy and program questions outlined in the beginning of this chapter during the first stage of our implementation.
4. It was impossible to pay too much attention to staff training and promotion of the program. Staff

understanding and buy-in of the program was the key to our success. They are the ambassadors of the program and mentor students in its use and application. Training needed to be intensive and ongoing; promotion needed to be extensive and engaging.

5. We were flexible enough to adapt the processes when they were not working as envisioned. We continued to embrace the basic principles of identifying and repairing harm and rebuilding trust but allowed for those things to happen in the most appropriate ways.

◇◇◇◇◇◇◇◇◇◇◇◇◇◇◇◇◇◇◇◇◇◇◇◇◇◇◇◇◇◇◇

Challenges to implementation

Starting an RJ program poses some dilemmas for campuses. One is the problem of case referrals. Most campuses are cautious about this new approach and wish to refer only the most minor cases. But those often have the least tangible harm, such as underage alcohol possession or marijuana possession.

RJ cases are most effective when they have clearly identifiable harms, which help the participants shift from the mindset of punishing code violations to repairing harm and rebuilding trust. So implementing a new program requires a small leap of faith in its first case referrals to ensure that more serious cases are included.

A similar leap of faith is required with facilitation and training. It is best to use experienced facilitators, but a new program will not have these. It is also best to use trainers that have facilitation and implementation experience, but again, a new program may not have such staff readily available. Partnerships with community-based RJ programs is one solution, working with training consultants is another, but campuses must work quickly and deliberately to develop internal capacity and expertise. The next chapter offers tips on how to offer an RJ training.

10.
Facilitating a Restorative Justice Training

A campus RJ training should help participants gain a thorough understanding of restorative justice principles and practices, strong facilitation skills, practical information about program implementation, and the satisfaction of having participated in an intellectually and emotionally rewarding training experience.

Because RJ elicits both moral dialogue and raw emotions, it is important to create an experiential training environment that feels realistic to participants. Most are not really sold on the idea of RJ until they have experienced it in role play or observed an actual case. While there is much information to be shared, it is best done through dialogue and active learning rather than through lecture or PowerPoint presentation.

Designing the training

How much training is necessary? This will vary according to four key constituencies, each requiring increasing levels of training.

"As a campus consultant, I am often asked to offer RJ training. We use film clips and storytelling to assist the group to understand that RJ is a process designed to problem-solve rather than punish. They must experience a shift in their ideas of accountability, fairness, and justice. To do this, we put them in simulation as early as possible. A good student dilemma is presented: a drunken joy ride, a stolen exam, or a racist harassment on social media. In small groups, we ask the participants to respond. Next we ask the groups to follow the RJ script and compare their outcomes. It is at once transformative.

Facilitator trainings teach participants how to convene a conference so the harm is represented, offering the best chance of a restorative outcome. Apprentices learn to trust the structure of the RJ process and the wisdom of those assembled to repair harm and rebuild trust. They learn to face harms objectively, post harms accurately, and understand the unmet needs represented by those harms. Once the needs are identified, plans and strategies to meet them are not far off. Training groups learn that with disciplined application of the RJ process and facilitation skills, complex situations can be made manageable and transformed to opportunities of personal growth and campus-wide healing."

Duke Fisher
Consultant/Trainer

RJ advocates are individuals who do not participate in the program but need to know enough about it to advocate for it. They might be a dean or professor or student leader. A few hours of training are probably sufficient for this group.

RJ facilitators must have a thorough understanding of RJ principles and facilitation skills in at least one method of practice (such as conferencing).

RJ program coordinators should be able to mentor facilitators as well as understand the nuts and bolts of program implementation from revising conduct codes to case management.

RJ trainers should have on-the-ground experience with case facilitation as well as a broad understanding of types of practices and the global landscape of restorative justice.

Below is a list of training topics and intended audiences. Each module is approximately three hours.

Many organizations provide training in restorative practices. Ideally, resources can be found locally by contacting community-based programs or faculty on campus.

Facilitating a Restorative Justice Training

Topic	Advocate	Facilitator	Coordinator	Trainer
Overview of RJ	√	√	√	√

Principles, practices, evidence of effectiveness, case studies

Topic	Advocate	Facilitator	Coordinator	Trainer
Introduction to Facilitation		√	√	√

Role of facilitator, sequence of process, preconference preparation, facilitation guide or script, role play

Topic	Advocate	Facilitator	Coordinator	Trainer
Identifying Harm		√	√	√

Listening and reflection skills, nuanced identification of harm and associated underlying needs, role play

Topic	Advocate	Facilitator	Coordinator	Trainer
RJ Outcomes		√	√	√

Collaborative brainstorming, apologies, restitution, community service, social justice initiatives, rebuilding trust

Topic	Advocate	Facilitator	Coordinator	Trainer
Issues in Facilitation		√	√	√

Diversity and inclusion, trauma-informed practice, denial of responsibility, multipartiality, role play

Topic	Advocate	Facilitator	Coordinator	Trainer
Implementation			√	√

Program models, referrals, case management, marketing a program, training, policy updates

Topic	Advocate	Facilitator	Coordinator	Trainer
Train-the-trainer				√

Active learning, lesson planning, practice and coaching

11.
Preparing for a Restorative Justice Conference

Most practitioners emphasize the importance of preparing people for participation in an RJ conference. Unlike mediation practice, where facilitators frequently know little about the dispute, RJ facilitators gather as much information as they can beforehand. This is necessary because the risk of revictimization is reduced when facilitators know the perspectives of the participants and what they are likely to say during the conference.

The RJ facilitator makes contact with all participants before the RJ conference in order to assess the appropriateness of holding the conference. The facilitator discusses the process of the conference and its potential value for the participants. The preconference process is an opportunity to build trust with the facilitator; discuss the questions that will be asked in the conference; explore various harms, needs, and concerns; and have all questions answered.

Preconference Meeting

For all participants: describe the conferencing process simply and clearly:
- This is a facilitated dialogue with the person responsible and harmed parties.
- It is an opportunity to talk about what happened and identify the harm caused by the incident and how it has affected people.
- The focus is on repairing harm and rebuilding trust, not on punishment or passing judgment.
- The participants will brainstorm how to repair harm, meet needs, and rebuild trust.
- It is a voluntary process.
- The facilitators are trained and multipartial (they will help everyone to have their perspective represented).
- It is confidential (explain caveats according to campus policy), except if there is imminent danger.
- The agreement, if signed, is binding.
- Outcomes might include actions to make things right, restitution, community service, demonstrating understanding of harm, and apologizing.
- Support people are invited to help make participants feel more comfortable and to assist them in getting the most out of the restorative conference.
- Share a little bit about yourself and why you are interested in being an RJ facilitator.

Get to know each participant as a person:
- What classes are they taking?
- What clubs or activities are they involved with on campus?

- Where are they from?
- What is their major?

Hear the story:
- Share that this is the moment to practice responding to what will be asked during the conference.
- Paraphrase/reflect feelings. Allow for silence. Listen for ability to express emotion. Listen for red flags (listed in next section) that would make case inappropriate for conferencing, especially denials of responsibility, risks of revictimization, and issues of mental health. Listen also for a willingness to engage restoratively.

Preconference questions for a person who has *caused harm*:

What happened?
At its core, RJ is a storytelling process. This question opens the door to manifesting the story. Both those who have been harmed and those who have caused harm want to be heard.

At the time, what were you thinking about?
This gives perspective and insight to a person's state of mind at the incident. It also can be important to assess the person's sense of remorse and willingness to take responsibility.

What have you thought about since?
This question prompts self-reflection and the possibility of change.

What impact has this had on you?

The person often needs a chance to share the effect of getting caught and their fears of what might happen to them. Before they feel heard about their immediate concerns about themselves, they are less likely to empathize with the harmed parties.

Who else has been impacted and in which way?

This question helps the person start to think restoratively. Make a list of the "whos." Make sure you understand the harm for each person and what their needs might be.

What do you think you could you have done differently?

In line with motivational interviewing, this question helps the person focus on behavioral change and their decision-making process.

What needs to happen to make things right?

This question pivots the coaching session from understanding to action. This is what sets RJ conversations apart from other kinds of mentoring. It often goes unasked because we can't see an answer. And yet we ask it anyway. How can the harm be repaired? What would you like to say to the harmed party? What needs must be addressed? How can we meet those needs?

How can we rebuild trust?

Separate from repairing harm, it is important to be seen as responsible and trustworthy. What can you do to show that you can be a positive and contributing member of the community? Are there personal issues that need to be addressed? Will people be reassured if you were in counseling? Is there something that you could do to demonstrate that you really understand the harm that you caused?

Are there things in this community that encourage incidents like this to happen that you would like to see addressed?

While the conference is designed to discuss the specific incident and how the person responsible can address the harms and needs, this question gives them an opportunity to consider larger cultural or campus issues (binge drinking, hazing, racism, sexism, etc.).

Preconference questions for a person who was harmed:

What happened?

At its core, RJ is a storytelling process. This question opens the door to manifesting the story. Both those who have been harmed and those who have caused harm want to be heard.

What impact did this incident have on you?

This is the chance to identify the varied harms.

What was the hardest thing about this?

This helps the harmed party identify what was most important. This moves from identifying harm to identifying underlying needs. "Because of this harm, do you have a need for . . . e.g., safety, restitution, belonging, etc.?"

If the person responsible were here, is there anything you would like to say to them or ask them?

This question helps identify unanswered questions and can begin the process of writing an impact statement or what the person would say during a conference.

Is there anything that could be done right now that would help you meet your needs?

This is an opportunity to explore local resources and strategies for self-healing.

Are there things in this community that encourage incidents like this to happen that you would like to see addressed?

While the conference is designed to discuss the specific incident and how the person responsible can address the harms and needs, this question creates an opportunity for the harmed party to consider larger cultural or campus issues (binge drinking, hazing, racism, sexism, etc.).

What would you like to see the other person do to repair the harm they have caused you?

Brainstorming helps provide clarity about needs and goals.

For all participants: Discuss concerns and present potential benefits of conferencing:
- Ask what concerns they may have.
- Identify what needs might be met by participating in this process.

Potential benefits for **person responsible**:

- Have direct input in the outcome of the process.
- Opportunity to explain what happened from your perspective.
- Chance to express remorse and take responsibility.
- Ability to share who you are beyond this one mistake.
- Learn about everyone's perspectives and concerns.
- Include support person of your choice who can help you get the most out of the experience.
- Potential benefits for **harmed parties**:
  - Opportunity to meet with person responsible in a safe environment, which is often helpful for harmed parties.
  - Chance to express how you were/are affected.
  - Receive information about the misconduct directly from person responsible.
  - Have direct input in the outcome of the process.
  - Include support person of your choice who can help you get the most out of the experience.
- Discuss whether they want to participate.
- Identify potential support person.
- Review seating plan for conference.
- Review who will be in attendance.
- Ask for their preference about who speaks first at the conference.
- Answer any additional questions.
- Get and provide contact information.
- Schedule tentative date, time, and location.

Red flags

It is the facilitators' job to decide if the case is appropriate for an RJ conference. The following is a short list of considerations. Of course, flags are never fully red—there are always gray areas that require thoughtful judgment.

Voluntary process: The conference should not go forward if the student or harmed parties feel coerced into participation. While this may seem easy to assess, many programs offer incentives such as not having the offense appear on the student's disciplinary record. Incentives are fine, but facilitators must assess whether or not participants feel unduly pressured.

Admission of responsibility: With the exception of RJ boards, restorative practices minimally expect that the student has admitted the misconduct. Even so, it is common for offenders to dispute some of the facts of the case to deny responsibility ("I was in possession of the stolen laptop, but I didn't steal it"), displace responsibility ("I stole the laptop, but it was my roommate's idea"), or diminish it ("It was an old laptop anyway, and their insurance company will replace it with a better one").

Some programs refer cases to RJ only when the student expresses deep remorse; others use the RJ process to help students understand the harm and learn to take full responsibility.

Victim safety: The goal of RJ is to help harmed parties, not cause further damage. Facilitators must keep this in mind during preconference meetings. Will the offender engage in victim-blaming? How fragile does the harmed party appear?

Mental health: Facilitators are not in a position to make clinical diagnoses, and RJ conferences are not designed as therapeutic interventions. Clear signs of mental illness are an indication that participants may not be able to listen effectively or be capable of representing themselves in a conference.

Willingness to engage restoratively: are the participants willing to work together; move beyond a punitive mindset; honor confidentiality; and focus on mutual understanding, repairing harm, and building community?

12.
Conference Facilitator Apprentice Script

Many RJ practitioners debate the value of using an RJ script. Some believe it is important to follow one closely to ensure consistent practice. For example, if one harmed party is asked a specific question like "What do you think needs to happen to make things right?" then it is important to ask another harmed party the same question. Other practitioners, however, like to rely on well-developed group facilitation skills that enable them to be responsive to the situation and guide the conversation in unplanned directions.

My solution to this is to provide an "apprentice script,"[1] which can be followed closely for those who want to rely on a clear set of prompts but which also (in the left column) highlights topics to be addressed to help practitioners maintain a coherent flow without binding them to particular questions. The script, of course, can always be adapted to best represent the style of the facilitators and customized to reflect campus norms or policies.

In general, the flow of dialogue is illustrated as follows. The pattern begins with the offender or "person responsible," who describes the incident first. Often, harmed parties are reticent to speak until they have first heard from the person responsible. In this script, the person responsible speaks first, but some facilitators will invite the participants to decide who will speak first. After the harmed parties speak, the flow returns to the person responsible again so that they can respond to what others have said. Ideally, the parties will be seated so that those who are most open to the restorative process speak first.

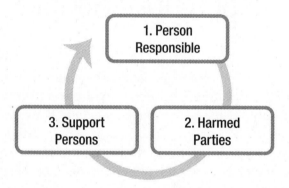

The next illustration is a guide to seating arrangements. The person responsible is placed close to a facilitator and their support person. Ideally, they are seated opposite to harmed parties, providing some distance between them, but they can also look at and speak directly to each other. The seating template also highlights a common division of labor between facilitators. One tends to open the conference, hosting the conversation while the other posts harms on a flip chart. However, as the dialogue shifts to the listing of harms and brainstorming solutions, the second facilitator usually takes over.

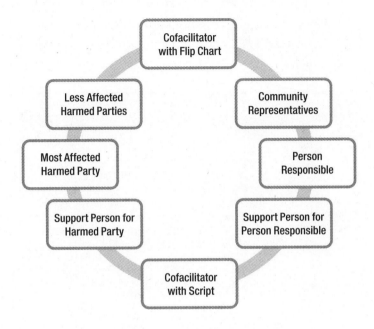

What to do right before the conference:

- Ensure that all your facilitation materials are ready (script, seating plan, flip chart and markers, pen/pads, incident summary, name tags).
- Before the participants arrive, arrange the chairs according to your seating plan.
- Be ready to greet the participants upon arrival and invite harmed parties and person responsible to wait in separate areas.
- When everyone is ready, invite the participants into the conference room and show them to their seats. Seat any observers and secondary stakeholders first, harmed parties next, and the person responsible last, especially if the conference is large.

- The following text includes suggested prompts and questions. Facilitators can modify as appropriate.

Introduction

Bulleted Script	Example Text
• Welcome and introductions	*To everybody:* Welcome everybody. Before the formal part of the conference begins, please silence your cell phones. The conference will last approximately two hours. I would like us to introduce ourselves and indicate briefly our reasons for being here. I am [cofacilitator's name], and I will be cofacilitating today's conference. Let's go around the circle. Please tell us your name and your connection to this conference today.
• Focus of conference	Thank you for attending. At today's conference, we will be focusing on the [incident]. Once we have learned more about what happened, we will identify what harm was caused and how it might be repaired. We will also focus on what can be done to reassure us that the behavior will not be repeated.
• Agreement to be approved by administration	This conference is voluntary. We do not have to reach an agreement today, and if we do not, the case will be referred back to the administration and handled in a different way. I am hopeful that we will reach an agreement, and if so, we will submit it to them for approval. It is possible, but rare, that they will want to make changes to the agreement. Does everybody understand this?

• Group norms	One goal of this conference is to create an environment in which everyone can speak freely and fully about how they feel about what happened. As facilitators, our job is to ensure that everyone here has a voice. Sometimes, we will have open dialogue in which everyone can participate as they wish; at other times, we will go around the circle inviting each person to offer their perspective. When we do, a person can always pass if they do not have anything they want to say at that time.

Another job for us as facilitators is to create an environment of trust, so that we can speak honestly about the incident. To enable this, will everyone agree that what is said in this circle will stay in the circle—that we will not talk about what people have said here to others? |
| • Background of person responsible | ***To person responsible:***
We would like to begin by getting to know you as a person and learn how you might be able to contribute to a positive resolution.
Which classes are you taking this semester?
What is your major?
How are you involved on campus? Clubs? Activities?
What do you hope will come of this discussion today?
Simply say, "thank you," after each person has spoken. |

Harm Identification

• Introduce harm identification	*Cofacilitator posts harms on a flip chart, asking for confirmation of accuracy and completeness. Facilitator can post harms after each person has spoken or wait until everyone has spoken. In either case, do not post offender harms first. Use clear, brief, specific language while flip-charting. Don't "smooth over" language, e.g., list "broken window," not "window," and "fear of walking outside at night," not "safe campus." Harms should be the length of "hashtags," e.g., #punched wall, #team mistrust. When listing harms, also highlight underlying needs. For example, if someone is afraid to walk outside at night, they might have a need for "safety." Brainstorming should focus on meeting that need.* **To everybody:** Now we will learn about the incident by asking everyone to tell us about what happened from their perspective. We will start with the person(s) responsible, then hear from harmed parties, and then support persons.
• Person responsible	**To person responsible (ask all of the questions in sequence before moving to next person):** Can you tell us what happened? At the time, what were you thinking about? What have you thought about since? What impact has this incident had on you? Who else has been affected by this incident and in what way? Is there anything else you would like to share or ask at this time? *Repeat for additional responsible parties, if any. Ask all of the questions even if you think they have been answered.*
• Harmed parties	**To harmed parties:** What happened from your perspective? What impact has this incident had on you? What has been the hardest thing about this? Is there anything else you would like to share or ask at this time?

84

• Support persons	**To support persons:** What brings you to the conference today? What has been the most difficult thing for you about this incident? What are the harms you would like to see addressed? Is there anything else you would like to share or ask at this time?
• Person responsible	**To person responsible:** You have now had a chance to hear about how the incident has affected everyone. Is there anything you would like to share at this time?
• Summarize harms and check for accuracy	*Facilitators may wish to shift primary leadership* *at this point and have the facilitator who has* *been listing harms lead the review of them and* *the brainstorming process to find solutions.* **To everybody:** We will now summarize our list of harms. Is there anything to be changed or added?

Agreement Process

• Solutions	*Start a new flip-chart page called "solutions."*
• Explore how to make things right	**To everybody:** We have all spoken about the harms caused by this incident and are now at the stage of identifying what can be done to make things right. A few questions will guide us forward. What is some- thing good that can come out of this difficult situation? What would that look like? How can harm be addressed? How can we best meet people's needs? How can we rebuild trust? Are we mean- ingfully addressing larger social concerns?

• Check for agreement to proceed	Considering these questions, would you like to look for solutions? *If not, then end the conference and refer back to the administration. Thank participants for their willingness to bring the details of the harm to light. Dismiss participants.*
• Break, if desired	*State the conference is about halfway done. Ask participants if they would like to take a short break before continuing. If you go on a break, it is okay if participants talk informally, but pay attention to the tone, and keep the break short. Offer snacks!*
• Introduce brainstorming	This next stage is about coming up with ideas. We will write all of the suggestions on the flip chart. Later, we can decide to make changes and finalize an agreement that is satisfactory to everyone. During this brainstorming process, we will post all of your ideas on the flip chart. Later, we can refine them and write up the agreement. Unlike the first half, the brainstorming phase can be less structured and more open to collaborative discussion of ideas.
• Ask how the harm could be repaired • Ask how trust can be restored	*To person responsible:* Looking at this list of harms, what do you think can be done to repair them? What else can you do to demonstrate that you can be a trusted and positive member of our community?
• Check with harmed parties for their ideas to repair the harm and regain trust	*To harmed parties sequentially, then support persons:* Looking at this list of harms, what do you think can be done to repair them? How can the plan help meet your needs? What else would you need to see from [*person responsible*] to restore your confidence in them?

• Check for collective agreement	***To everybody:*** What do you think of what we have come up with so far? Are we meaningfully responding to larger social concerns? Let's make sure we have a plan that best addresses our concerns and is also fair and reasonable.
• Communication with the wider community	How can we best communicate this outcome to the wider community?
• Check back with person responsible	***To person responsible:*** Would you be able to agree to these suggestions? Do you have any concerns about the plan that we should address?
• Address administrative review	***To everybody:*** Now that we have reached an agreement, we will submit it to the administration for approval.
• Share consequences if agreement is not fulfilled	***To everybody:*** [Person responsible] will have to complete the various tasks by the deadline or [explain consequences, e.g, not able to register for next semester's classes].
• Appeals process	***To person responsible:*** If after you leave, you believe that this process was conducted unfairly, you can appeal the agreement we have reached with the administration.

Closing

	Try to end on a positive note by expressing appreciation for the hard work completed.
• Final round—how are you feeling about how things went?	***To everybody:*** Thank you for your hard work today. In closing this conference, I'd like to go around the circle and ask each person how they are feeling about how things went. I'll start by saying . . .

13.
Final Thoughts

"Out beyond ideas of wrongdoing and rightdoing,
there is a field. I will meet you there."

                              Jalal al-Din Rumi[1]

Several years ago, a student in my criminal justice class was living off campus, and her house was burglarized. She was home asleep, and her three housemates were out. She never heard or saw the offender, but several items were taken. A few nights later, the four friends—all female—were hanging out in their living room and were startled when they saw a man staring through the window, watching them.

Of course, they called the police and their parents. The students were quite frightened, and they began to sleep elsewhere at night—sometimes leaving only one of them alone who had not made other plans. Their self-protective efforts were not well coordinated. The lock on the front door was broken, and they were having trouble getting a response from the landlord to fix it.

They went to our Dean of Student Affairs, who told them that since they lived off campus, there wasn't anything the college could do for them except refer them to the counseling center. Because they were adults and had chosen to live off campus, it was up to them to take the necessary steps to protect themselves and negotiate with the landlord.

At this point, they all wanted to move out and to renegotiate the lease. The dean said that the offender, who had not been caught, was not likely to be another student, so this was really a police matter.

We discussed these responses in class, and all agreed that what the dean said was true, but it didn't seem very helpful. It didn't meet the needs of the students. I asked them what justice required, and their first response was to find the perpetrator. Maybe the police should stake out the place and double their efforts to catch the person. Then he should be put in jail. But, in the absence of an offender, they did not see a way for justice to be achieved.

Because we were reading about restorative justice, I pointed out that our criminal justice system is very offender-centered. All of our energy is devoted to finding criminals and punishing them—the "trail 'em, nail 'em, jail 'em" approach to justice.

Restorative justice is different because it is balanced between its attention to offenders and to victims. It is different because it is a harm-centered approach. The first questions that are asked are different. Instead of "Who did it, and what should we do to them?" restorative justice asks, "What is the harm, and how can it be repaired?"

Reframing the question in this way, I asked the class again, "What could be a just response to our classmate's predicament?" This time, the class immediately focused on her needs in the moment. She felt unsafe. She felt trapped in a housing situation that she did not want to be in.

After a period of brainstorming, the class agreed that they wanted to help. They encouraged her to continue working with the landlord to be released from the housing contract. One person in the class said that he knew how to change a lock, and if the housemates would pay for the parts, he would come over that day and take care of it.

The group decided that they did not want any of the housemates to spend another night alone in the house and encouraged the student to create a schedule with her roommates so all would know the plans of the others. And they committed to taking turns calling the classmate each night to make sure she was not alone and decided that one of them would go over and spend the night if she was.

These students found creative and meaningful solutions for their fellow classmate and crime victim. It was also a learning opportunity for them to refocus their attention from offender to victim and from punishment to community building. In that field beyond wrongdoing and "rightdoing," they found a new kind of justice that involved them in a creative problem-solving process, actively engaged their participation, taught them how to apply their generosity and goodwill, and enabled them to offer real, practical assistance to a friend in need.

Restorative justice offers student conduct programs a disciplinary response that is frequently a transformative learning opportunity for all students, whether they have caused harm or been affected by it. For students who have caused harm, it offers a real chance for personal growth. As our STARR Project findings demonstrated, they can leave this process believing they will be treated fairly, they will have a voice in the outcome, they can courageously talk it out with the people they affected, they can take active responsibility for making things right, and that they have a place on campus where they can succeed.

Endnotes

Introduction: The Story of the Spirit Horse

[1] An earlier version of this case study appeared in *Student Affairs eNews*, December 20, 2011.

[2] Melton, Ada Pecos. "Indigenous Justice Systems and Tribal Society," in *Judicature* 79 (1995):126–133.

Chapter 2: The Principles of Restorative Justice

[1] While I sometimes use the term "offender" to refer to someone who has caused harm, many restorative practitioners use other phrases, such as "person who caused harm" to highlight how terms like "offender" or "perpetrator" can be stigmatizing.

[2] Bazemore, Gordon. "Restorative Justice and Earned Redemption," in *American Behavioral Scientist* 41 (1998):768–813.

[3] Braithwaite, John and Declan Roche. "Responsibility and Restorative Justice," in *Restorative Community Justice: Repairing Harm and Transforming Communities,* edited by Gordon Bazemore and Mara Schiff (Cincinnati, OH: Anderson, 2001), 63–84.

Chapter 3: Restorative Justice in the Model Student Conduct Code

[1] Akchurin, Roane, Joyce Ester, Pricilla Mori, and Amy Van Meter. "Conferencing Case Study: The Lounge, Leg Hair, and Learning," in *Restorative Justice on the College Campus: Promoting Student Growth and Responsibility, and Reawakening the Spirit of Campus Community,* edited by David R. Karp and Thom Allena (Springfield, IL: Charles C Thomas, 2004), 70–76.

2 Pavela, Gary. "Limiting the 'Pursuit of Perfect Justice' on Campus: A Proposed Code of Student Conduct," in *The Journal of College and University Law* 6 (1979–1980):137–160.

3 Stoner, Edward N. and John W. Lowery. "Navigating Past the 'Spirit of Insubordination': A Twenty-First Century Model Student Conduct Code with a Model Hearing Script," in *Journal of College and University Law* 31 (2004):1–77.

4 Dean, Laura A. *CAS Professional Standards for Higher Education,* 7th edition (Washington, D.C.: Council for the Advancement of Standards in Higher Education, 2009), 359.

5 Pavela, Gary. *Law and Policy Report* 334, Association for Student Conduct Administration, October 1, 2009.

6 Braithwaite, John. *Restorative Justice and Responsive Regulation* (New York: Oxford University Press, 2002).

7 For an extended analysis of differences between a restorative justice conference and a model code hearing, see David R. Karp, "Reading the Scripts: The Restorative Justice Conference and the Student Conduct Hearing Board," in *Reframing Campus Conflict: Student Conduct Process through a Social Justice Lens,* edited by Jennifer Meyer Schrage and Nancy Geist Giacomini (Sterling, VA: Stylus Publishers, 2009), 155–174.

Chapter 4: Three Models of Campus Practice

1 Maloney, Dennis. 2007. "A Sense of Justice." YouTube Video. https://www.youtube.com/watch?v=Y7MhQG5BiYQ.

2 Jelinek, Libby. "Program to Revamp Student Justice," in *The Vista,* October 13, 2011, available at http://www.theusdvista.com/news/program-to-revamp-student-justice-1.2647643?pagereq=1.

3 This case was described to me by Rick Shafer, Associate Director of Student Life, Michigan State University.

4 Conversation with the author.

5 Wachtel, Joshua. "Healing After a Student Suicide: Restorative Circles at the University of Vermont," in *Restorative Practices E-Forum,* February 12, 2011, available at http://www.iirp.edu/article_detail.php?article_id=Njg4.

Chapter 6: Best Practices in Repairing Harm and Rebuilding Trust

1   Ross, Rupert. *Returning to the Teachings: Exploring Aboriginal Justice* (New York: Penguin, 1996), 175.

2   Conversation with the author.

3   Yellow Horse Brave Heart, Maria. 1998. "The Return to the Sacred Path: Healing the Historical Trauma and Historical Unresolved Grief Response among the Lakota through a Psychoeducational Group Intervention," in *Smith College Studies in Social Work* 68:3: 287–305.

4   McMahon, Sheila M., David R. Karp, and Hayley Mulhern. "Addressing Individual and Community Needs in the Aftermath of Campus Sexual Misconduct: Restorative Justice as a Way Forward in the Re-Entry Process," in *Journal of Sexual Aggression*. (2018) DOI: 10.1080/13552600.2018.1507488.

5   Conversation with the author.

Chapter 7: Does It Work? Research and Assessment of Campus Restorative Programs

1   Karp, David R. and Megan Schachter. "Restorative Justice in Colleges and Universities: What Works When Addressing Student Misconduct." Pp. 247–263 in *The Routledge Handbook of Restorative Justice*, edited by Theo Gavrielides (New York: Routledge, 2018).

2   For an elaboration of STARR Project research findings, see Karp and Sacks, "Research Findings on Restorative Justice and Alcohol Violations," and Karp and Sacks, "Student Conduct, Restorative Justice, and Student Development."

3   The data show mean satisfaction scores for 135 restorative justice cases.

4   Each dimension was constructed by multiple indicators.

Chapter 8: Restorative Justice and Social Justice

1   Koss, Mary P., Jay K. Wilgus, and Kaaren M. Williamsen. 2014. "Campus Sexual Misconduct: Restorative Justice Approaches to Enhance Compliance with Title IX Guidance." *Trauma, Violence & Abuse* 15: 242–257.

2   Acosta, David and David R. Karp. 2017. "Restorative Justice as the Rx for Mistreatment in Academic Medicine: Applications to

Consider for Learners, Faculty and Staff." *Academic Medicine* 93: 354–356. DOI: 10.1097/ACM.0000000000002037.

3 Anderson, Desiree. 2018. *The Use of Campus Based Restorative Justice Practices to Address Incidents of Bias: Facilitators' Experiences*. University of New Orleans Theses and Dissertations. 2442.

4 Mok, Harry. "UC Explores Restorative Justice in Improving Campus Climate," in *UC Newsroom*, January 27, 2012, available at http://www.universityofcalifornia.edu/news/article/27045.

5 Conversation with the author.

6 Peterson, Marilyn R Armour. *At Person Risk: Boundary Violations in Professional-Client Relationships* (New York: W. W. Norton, 1992).

Chapter 9: A Whole-Campus Approach to Implementation

1 Armour, Marilyn. 2016. "Restorative Practices: Righting the Wrongs of Exclusionary School Discipline." *University of Richmond Law Review*. 50: 999–1037.

2 McMahon, Sheila M., David R. Karp, and Hayley Mulhern. 2018. "Addressing Individual and Community Needs in the Aftermath of Campus Sexual Misconduct: Restorative Justice as a Way Forward in the Re-Entry Process." *Journal of Sexual Aggression*. DOI: 10.1080/13552600.2018.1507488.

Chapter 12: Conference Facilitator Apprentice Script

1 This script is based on conferencing scripts by Sandy Bowles, Guilford College; Chris Dinnan, Vermont Department of Corrections; Charles Barton, *Restorative Justice: The Empowerment Model*; and Terry O'Connell et al., *Conferencing Handbook: The New Real Justice Training Manual*.

Chapter 13: Final Thoughts

1 Rumi, Jalal al-Din. *The Essential Rumi*, Coleman Barks, translator (New York: HarperOne, 2004).

Resources

Website: www.CampusRJ.org

A website that provides general resources for campus restorative justice, including links to publications and training opportunities.

David Karp's publications focusing on campus restorative justice

Karp, David R. "Restorative Justice and Responsive Regulation in Higher Education: The Complex Web of Campus Sexual Assault Policy in the United States and a Restorative Alternative." In *Restorative and Responsive Human Services*, edited by Gale Burford, Valerie Braithwaite, and John Braithwaite (New York: Routledge, 2019).

Karp, David R. and Megan Schachter. "Restorative Justice in Colleges and Universities: What Works When Addressing Student Misconduct." In *The Routledge Handbook of Restorative Justice,* edited by Theo Gavrielides (New York: Routledge, 2018).

McMahon, Sheila M., David R. Karp, and Hayley Mulhern. 2018. "Addressing Individual and Community Needs in the Aftermath of Campus Sexual Misconduct: Restorative Justice as a Way Forward in the Re-Entry Process." *Journal of Sexual Aggression.* DOI: 10.1080/13552600.2018.1507488.

Acosta, David and David R. Karp. 2017. "Restorative Jus-
tice as the Rx for Mistreatment in Academic Medicine:
Applications to Consider for Learners, Faculty and
Staff." *Academic Medicine* 93: 354–356. DOI: 10.1097/
ACM.0000000000002037.

Karp, David R. and Olivia Frank. 2016. "Anxiously Await-
ing the Future of Restorative Justice in the United
States." *Victims & Offenders* 11: 50–70.

Karp, David R., Julie Shackford-Bradley, Robin J. Wilson,
and Kaaren M. Williamsen. *Campus PRISM: A Report
on Promoting Restorative Initiatives for Sexual Misconduct
on College Campuses* (Saratoga Springs, NY: Skidmore
College Project on Restorative Justice, 2016).

Karp, David R. and Olivia Frank. "Restorative justice and
student development in higher education: Expanding
'offender' horizons beyond punishment and rehabilitation to community engagement and personal growth,"
in *Offenders No More: New Offender Rehabilitation
Theory and Practice*, edited by Theo Gavrielides (New
York: Nova Science Publishers, 2015).

Karp, David R. "Restorative Justice at Dalhousie: A Rea-
soned Alternative to the 'Rush to Judgment,'" in *Association for Student Conduct Administration Law and Policy
Report.* January 29, 2015.

Karp, David R. and Casey Sacks. "Student Conduct,
Restorative Justice, and Student Development: Findings
from the STARR Project (Student Accountability and
Restorative Research Project)," in *Contemporary Justice
Review.* 17 (2014): 154–172.

Karp, David R. and Casey Sacks. "Research Findings
on Restorative Justice and Alcohol Violations," in
*NASPA Alcohol and Other Drug Knowledge Community
Newsletter* Fall 2012.

Karp, David R. "Spirit Horse and the Principles of Restorative Justice," in *Student Affairs eNews* December 20, 2011.

Karp, David R. "Not with a Bang but a Whimper: A Missed Opportunity for Restorative Justice in a Plagiarism Case," in *Journal of Student Conduct Administration* 2(1) (2009):26–30.

Karp, David R. "Reading the Scripts: The restorative Justice Conference and the Student Conduct hearing Board," in *Reframing Campus Conflict: Student Conduct Process through a Social Justice Lens*, edited by Jennifer Meyer Schrage and Nancy Geist Giacomini (Sterling, VA: Stylus, 2009).

Karp, David R. "Campus Justice is Behind the Times," in *Inside Higher Ed* October 28, 2005.

Karp, David R. and Suzanne Conrad. "Restorative Justice and College Student Misconduct," in *Public Organization Review* 5 (2005):315-333.

Karp, David R. and Thom Allena, eds. *Restorative Justice on the College Campus: Promoting Student Growth and Responsibility, and Reawakening the Spirit of Campus Community* (Springfield, IL: Charles C. Thomas, 2004).

Restorative justice books in the Little Books of Justice and Peacebuilding series

Davis, Fania E. *The Little Book of Race and Restorative Justice* (New York, NY: Good Books, 2019).

Norman, Dewolfe Thomas and Jodie Geddes. *The Little Book of Racial Healing* (New York, NY: Good Books, 2019).

Friesen, Julie and Wendy Meek. *The Little Book of Restorative Justice for Older Adults* (New York, NY: Good Books, 2017).

Evans, Katherine and Dorothy Vaandering. *The Little Book of Restorative Justice in Education* (New York, NY: Good Books, 2016).

Hooker, David Anderson. *The Little Book of Transformative Community Conferencing* (New York, NY: Good Books, 2016).

Lederach, John Paul. *The Little Book of Conflict Transformation* (New York, NY: Good Books, 2015).

Oudshoorn, Judah, Lorraine Stutzman Amstutz, and Michelle Jackett. *The Little Book of Restorative Justice for Sexual Abuse* (New York, NY: Good Books, 2015).

Pranis, Kay. *The Little Book of Circle Processes* (Intercourse, PA: Good Books, 2005).

Stutzman Amstutz, Lorraine and Judy H. Mullet. *The Little Book of Restorative Discipline for Schools* (New York, NY: Good Books, 2015).

Yoder, Carolyn. *The Little Book of Trauma Healing* (New York, NY: Good Books, 2015).

Zehr, Howard. *The Little Book of Restorative Justice* (New York, NY: Good Books, 2015).

Zehr, Howard, Allan MacRae, Kay Pranis, and Lorraine Stutzman Amstutz. *The Big Book of Restorative Justice* (New York, NY: Good Books, 2015).

Stutzman Amstutz, Lorraine. *The Little Book of Victim Offender Conferencing* (New York, NY: Good Books, 2009).

MacRae, Allan and Howard Zehr. *The Little Book of Family Group Conferences, New Zealand Style* (Intercourse, PA: Good Books, 2004).

Toews, Barbara. *The Little Book of Restorative Justice for People in Prison* (Intercourse, PA: Good Books, 2006).

Other important restorative justice books

Boyes-Watson, Carolyn and Kay Pranis. *Circle Forward: Building a Restorative School Community*. (St. Paul, MN: Living Justice Press, 2015).

Braithwaite, John. *Restorative Justice and Responsive Regulation* (New York: Oxford University Press, 2002).

Pranis, Kay, Barry Stuart, and Mark Wedge. *Peacemaking Circles* (St. Paul, MN: Living Justice Press, 2003).

Ross, Rupert. *Returning to the Teachings: Exploring Aboriginal Justice* (New York: Penguin, 1996).

Schrage, Jennifer Meyer and Nancy Geist Giacomini, eds. *Reframing Campus Conflict: Student Conduct Process through a Social Justice Lens* (Sterling, VA: Stylus, 2009).

Sered, Danielle. 2019. *Until We Reckon: Violence, Mass Incarceration, and a Road to Repair*. New York: New Press.

Thorsborne, Margaret and Peta Blood. *Implementing Restorative Practices in Schools* (Philadelphia, PA: Jessica Kingsley, 2013).

Umbreit, Mark and Marilyn Peterson Armour. *Restorative Justice Dialogues: A Research-Based Approach to Working with Victims, Offenders, Families, and Communities* (New York: Springer, 2010).

Zehr, Howard. *Change Lenses* (Scottdale, PA: Herald Press, 1990).

About the Author

David Karp is a professor in the School of Leadership and Education Sciences at the University of San Diego. His current scholarship focuses on restorative justice in community and educational settings. He was the recipient of the Donald D. Gehring Award from the Association for Student Conduct Administration for his work on campus restorative justice. David has published more than one hundred academic papers and six books, including *Wounds That Do Not Bind: Victim-Based Perspectives on the Death Penalty* and *The Community Justice Ideal*. David serves on the Board of Directors for the National Association for Community and Restorative Justice. He has previously served as Associate Dean of Student Affairs and Professor of Sociology at Skidmore College. David received a BA in Peace and Conflict Studies from the University of California at Berkeley and a PhD in Sociology from the University of Washington.

Group Discounts for

The Little Book of
Restorative Justice
for Colleges and Universities
ORDER FORM

If you would like to order multiple copies of *The Little Book of Restorative Justice for Colleges and Universities* by David Karp for groups you know or are a part of, please email **bookorders@skyhorsepublishing.com** or fax order to **(212) 643-6819**. (Discounts apply only for more than one copy.) Photocopy this page and the next as often as you like.

The following discounts apply:

1 copy	$5.99
2-5 copies	$5.39 each (a 10% discount)
6-10 copies	$5.09 each (a 15% discount)
11-20 copies	$4.79 each (a 20% discount)
21-99 copies	$4.19 each (a 30% discount)
100 or more	$3.59 each (a 40% discount)

Free Shipping for orders of 100 or more!
Prices subject to change.

Quantity   *Price*   *Total*

____ copies of *The Little Book of Restorative Justice*

for Colleges and Universities @ _____ _____

(Standard ground shipping costs will be added for orders of less than 100 copies.)

METHOD OF PAYMENT

❏   Check or Money Order
         (*payable to **Skyhorse Publishing** in U.S. funds*)

❏   Please charge my:
   ❏ MasterCard   ❏ Visa
   ❏ Discover ❏ American Express

\# _____

Exp. date and sec. code_____

Signature _____

Name _____

Address _____

City_____

State _____

Zip_____

Phone _____

Email _____

SHIP TO: (if different)
Name _____

Address _____

City_____

State _____

Zip_____

Call: (212) 643-6816
Fax: (212) 643-6819
Email: bookorders@skyhorsepublishing.com
(do not email credit card info)